VICTORIAN
MANSION
FLOWER SHOP
MYSTERIES

D0426367

# A Fatal Arrangement

Gayle Roper

Annie's®
AnniesFiction.com

## Books in the Victorian Mansion Flower Shop Mysteries series

Library of Congress-in-Publication Data
*A Fatal Arrangement* / by Gayle Roper
p. cm.
I. Title
                    2017943280

AnniesFiction.com
(800) 282-6643
Victorian Mansion Flower Shop Mysteries™
Series Creators: Shari Lohner, Janice Tate
Series Editors: Janice Tate, Ken Tate
Cover Illustrator: Kelley McMorris

10 11 12 13 14 I Printed in China I 9 8 7 6 5 4

# 1

"I'm really sorry, Dr. Bleu." Dr. Meninger, the head of the botany department, spoke without a trace of the regret he claimed.

Kaylee swallowed her disbelief and dismay. *Never let them see you bleed.* Hadn't someone somewhere said that?

"Budget cuts, you know." Dr. Meninger smiled pleasantly, the picture of collegial civility.

Kaylee responded automatically, though inside she felt hollow. Her life had just imploded and he was blaming it on budget cuts? *Ha!* It was politics, pure and simple. She knew that as well as she knew her name. She also knew there was nothing she could do to change the situation.

There had been one tenured position opened by the retirement of old Dr. Howson, and Kaylee had expected it to be hers. After all, she had a solid reputation as a teacher, and because of her PhD in plant taxonomy, she had become an expert witness for the Seattle Police Department in homicide cases, earning herself—and by extension the university—a certain notoriety. Students came to the University of Washington because they read about her testimony bringing criminals to justice.

What she had thought was a great mark in her favor had been turned against her by jealous colleagues. "Prima donna," were the whispers. "She thinks she's better than the rest of us. Asks for special concessions, you know."

Untrue, as anyone who knew her would testify, but how could she refute such accusations without sounding like the demanding braggart of the rumors? She couldn't, especially since she was fairly sure they'd been started by her main competition for the professorship. So she held her tongue, going for civility and maturity in spite of her deep distress at the character assassination. She had been certain Dr. Meninger would see beyond cheap gossip and false accusations.

"It's like being hit right between the eyes," she told her grandmother when they talked on the phone that evening. "My world is spinning out of control, and I'm so dizzy I can't see where I'm going anymore."

"Honey, you did right deciding to behave with such class," Beatrice Lyons said. "I'm proud of you."

"Thanks." Kaylee hit speaker on her phone and collapsed on the sofa in her tidy, colorful apartment. "But I've never been unemployed before. I've certainly never been fired. Or 'let go,' as he put it. I don't know how to behave. It's embarrassing."

"Head high, Katherine Leigh. You have nothing to be ashamed about."

"I can hold my head up all I want, but what do I do with all the hours in the day?"

"Relax, my girl. Have fun. Enjoy life. You've been working hard for so many years, first for your doctorate and then to be ready for that tenured position. It's time to find yourself."

"But I wasn't lost until today. I knew what I wanted and where I was going. It's only now that I don't know who I am. I mean, if I can't be a professor at the university I love, what can I be?"

Bear, her adorable dachshund, heard the despair in her voice and stood on his hind legs with his front paws on her knees. He looked at her with great concern—or at least that's what Kaylee read in his eyes.

"It's okay, Bear. Really." Kaylee fondled his silky ears. "Or at least it will be someday. I think." She sighed. "I hope."

He didn't look convinced, but after a lick on her hand he lay down with his head on her foot.

"I have a solution to your problem," Bea said.

"I'm glad someone does. I'm listening."

"You can take over The Flower Patch."

Kaylee frowned. "What? The Flower Patch is your life."

Bea sighed. "I'm tired, Kaylee. It's been so hard since your grandfather died, and I just don't have the energy or the enthusiasm to keep the shop going."

"Oh, Grandma." Kaylee immediately felt guilty for dumping her problems on her grandmother and more than slightly unnerved to hear the distress in the normally stoic woman's voice. She knew—everybody knew—the past five years had been hard for Bea without her husband, Edmond Lyons, especially given the mysterious circumstances of his death. Ed had gone out alone in his small skiff, not an unusual circumstance for someone living on an island, but he'd never returned. The skiff was later discovered floating loose in the Sound. No one was aboard, nor was his body ever found.

"Don't you go feeling sorry for me. I can't stand pity. I'm a widow, not an invalid."

Kaylee smiled. The starch was back in Bea's voice, and Kaylee's world was righted, at least that part of it. Bea's grit and courage were legendary in the family and were the reason Kaylee's parents had felt free to move to Florida to be near their son and his family, which included their two grandchildren.

"You taking over The Flower Patch and living in Wildflower Cottage is the solution to both our problems," Bea continued. "I've been so sad at the idea of a stranger buying my home and my business. Crazy, I know, but both places are so personal, so special to me. They hold such memories. Wouldn't it be wonderful if you were there to embrace those memories, to love them as much as I do? And you'd make your own to add to the line. Family. Continuity."

Kaylee could hear the longing in her grandmother's voice. She squeezed her eyes closed. Did she want to operate a flower shop on Orcas Island. "It's a lovely idea, Grandma, a really lovely idea, but I don't think so."

"I've surprised you."

That was an understatement. "You have. If you feel so strongly about it, why are you moving to Arizona?"

"I'm an old woman, and it's time."

"You're not old." Kaylee quickly did the math. She was forty, her mom was sixty, so her grandmother was in her eighties. *Yikes!* She was so vibrant and full of life that Kaylee often forgot just how old she was.

"At least promise me you'll consider the possibility," her grandmother urged.

Kaylee saw the flower shop in her mind's eye . . . the coolers full of colorful blooms, the scarred workbench in the design studio where Bea made her beautiful arrangements, like the decorative wreaths she created from dried flowers and grapevines. Kaylee could still smell the wonderful aroma of the fresh flowers, a fragrance that evoked memories of golden days helping her grandmother in the shop. She saw herself as a child sweeping up the stripped leaves, snipped buds, and clipped stems that always littered the workroom floor and, as she grew older, creating arrangements with her grandmother's help.

"I've been teaching you how to be a florist all your life," Bea said, her voice persuasive.

"True. I acquired my love of all things flora from you and my love of reading from Grandpa."

"Think about it, honey. That's all I ask. Whatever you decide, I'm moving to Arizona to live with Lucille. These joints of mine need dry heat, and this heart needs time with my twin."

One of several sticking points jumped out at Kaylee. "You said you're selling both The Flower Patch and Wildflower Cottage?"

"I have to. They'll provide my retirement funds. I wish I could give them to you, but I can't afford to do that."

"Of course you can't. I just don't think I can afford to buy them."

"Don't let it worry you. I'm sure we can work out a good deal, one you can afford and I can live with."

After they hung up, Kaylee thought for a long time. She had vivid memories of visits to her grandparents on Orcas Island. Somehow, the place had always felt like home, even though she had never lived there. She would still be working with plants, and she would feel closer to family residing in her beloved grandparents' home and continuing the business her grandmother had built.

*Maybe it's time for something new.*

# 2

One Monday in late June, Kaylee made her way to the main deck of the Washington State Ferry, where she leaned on the rail and turned her face to the wind. Who'd have thought losing her job would turn into such a great and unexpected adventure?

Granted, it wasn't an Indiana Jones escapade. Not many academics—or ex-academics in her case—raced around the world besting bad guys. Certainly no one would make a movie about her, but she was very happy with her normal-size adventure, one that was blissfully lacking in the politics and pressure of academia.

She grinned at the bald eagle that sailed overhead, wings spread wide. Feeling slightly foolish but unable to resist, she extended her arms in imitation. She laughed as the wind caught her jacket and pulled it away from her body so that she had wings too.

"Orcas Island," boomed the ferry's public address system.

At hearing the announcement, Kaylee's stomach gave a little flip—part excitement, part apprehension. The time had come to take that first big step in her adventure.

She followed the other passengers planning to disembark on Orcas down the steps to the car deck and walked between the vehicles until she reached her red Ford Escape. She slid behind the wheel and looked at her passenger.

"You ready, Bear?"

The little dachshund, who had been sound asleep on his favorite blanket until she opened the door, looked at her with a disgruntled expression.

"It's not my fault you had to stay in the car." She reached

out and scratched him behind an ear. "I told you it's the rule and one I can't change."

Bear leaned into her scratch but still radiated you-left-me displeasure. His bow tie had been knocked crooked by his napping position and the chest protector of his doggie seat belt.

The ferry slid into its slip, and all around her cars leaped to life. Slowly they pulled forward and off, Kaylee in the center of the stream. Orcas was the largest of the many San Juan Islands and the one Kaylee was most familiar with. Her grandparents had lived on the island as long as she could remember.

"You're going to love it here, Bear." She laughed out loud, something she hadn't done for weeks. She drove into Turtle Cove on the shore of West Sound, the smaller of the two arms of water that ate into the island. "*We're* going to love it here."

Bear appeared somewhat skeptical, but she knew he'd change his mind as soon as he realized how wonderful their new life was going to be. For one thing, he wouldn't have to be alone all day since she planned to take him to work with her. He was such a people dog—he'd love being the shop mascot.

The town looked much the same as it had the last time she'd seen it some twenty years ago. A couple of the shops had been repainted, and there were new signs at High Tide Outfitters, the village's sports outfitter, and Between the Lines, the bookstore located across the street and down from The Flower Patch. Up and down the street, flower boxes burst with blooms, yards were alive with color, and full hanging baskets of red and white petunias hung from the artsy light posts that lined the street. The moist, temperate climate made for wonderful growing conditions.

She pulled to the curb and sat staring at the impressive Victorian mansion that housed The Flower Patch. She leaned forward, studying the sign that hung above the porch, gold leaf spelling out the shop's name against a deep green background.

*My shop.* "Unbelievable."

Bear looked at her, confused. He gave a bark. He was ready to go. That was the way it worked. You stopped the car. You got out. You went somewhere.

"Okay, my friend. You deserve to get out of the car. You've been a very good boy."

Bear sat as Kaylee walked around the front of the car. When she reached for the door's handle, he stood, tail wagging, waiting impatiently for his seat belt to be taken off and the lead to be attached. Once that was done, he jumped out and ran in little circles, happy to be free again.

"Are you ready to see our shop?" As she said the words *our shop*, Kaylee felt her shoulders straighten and her breath catch. She was a business owner.

They walked up the steps to the big Victorian's wraparound porch where planters bursting with color hung above the porch railings. Just before she opened the door, Kaylee leaned down and adjusted the green plaid bow tie Bear wore, which matched her blazer. Not that she regularly dressed in outfits to match her dog—she wasn't quite that eccentric—but she did want to make a good first impression, and the green in the plaid made her eyes seem greener and Bear more handsome.

She pushed open the door and smiled at the tinkle of bells overhead. She'd loved that sound as a child. Grandpa Ed had once told her that the bells were a warning to the fairies who lived in the flowers, telling them to hide because someone had come into the shop.

A display against the west wall immediately caught Kaylee's eye. A huge photo of a bride holding one of Bea's beautiful bouquets hung suspended. Over the bride's shoulder was a huge urn full of flowers in shades of pink, cream, and blue. A bridesmaid stood in the distance, carrying a gorgeous nosegay in the same shades. At her side stood an adorable flower girl with a smaller nosegay and a wreath of colorful flowers in her hair.

The urn, full of the silk flowers featured in the photo, sat beside the photo, while on the other side a shiny white stepladder held small bouquets with trailing ribbons, a glittering tiara, and bejeweled dress sandals. All the items rested on a sweep of pink netting.

If that visual didn't make a prospective bride drool, nothing would.

"Kaylee!" A smiling woman with a chin-length gray-and-white bob and dark notice-me glasses walked around the counter with her arms extended. "I wasn't sure you'd be in today. I thought you might go straight to the house."

Kaylee smiled as the friendly stranger grasped both of her hands. "You must be Mary."

"Mary Bishop. I'm so glad to finally meet you. I've heard so much about you." Her gaze dropped to Bear. "And look at you! Aren't you the cutest thing?"

Bear's ears perked up, and he trotted closer for a good petting. Mary scratched under his chin. "I love your tie."

"So does he." Kaylee grinned at the tail-wagging Bear. "He's a terrible ham but a total charmer."

"Is this Bea's granddaughter?" called a lovely, petite woman with short, dark hair, a big smile, and a touch of Asian ancestry. She approached with hand outstretched. "I'm Jessica Roberts." Kaylee guessed Jessica was about the same age she was. The woman balanced stems of *Gerbera jamesonii* and *Asparagus setaceus* in one hand. "I own Death by Chocolate, the bakery and coffee shop next door." She indicated the gerbera daisies and asparagus ferns in her hand. "For my tables. Having you next door is so handy. I'm also a Petal."

"A Petal?"

Jessica laughed. "I guess Bea didn't tell you. It's short for Petal Pushers, our West Sound garden club. There's a bigger, island-wide garden club on Orcas, but we also have our little local one. Bea is a founding member."

"We hope you'll join us." Mary brushed her hair off her forehead. "We'd love your expertise."

"We meet Tuesdays in the keeper's quarters at the Old Cape Lighthouse," Jessica said. "I usually bring something chocolate, and Mary brings the hot drinks."

Kaylee wondered just how much gardening the group got done or even discussed. "In that case, I'm in. Thanks for including me, Jessica."

"Make that Jess. Jessica sounds so formal."

Kaylee smiled. "Okay. Jess it is."

"A new Petal. Wonderful." Mary gestured to an enticing stack of skin care products on the counter. "DeeDee Wilcox, the woman who crafts those wonderful lavender goat-milk soaps and creams, is in the club too. She owns the mystery bookstore across the street and down the way."

Kaylee looked out the front window at the store with its window boxes filled with rose geraniums, blue lobelia, and chartreuse sweet potato vines. "I look forward to meeting her. How many people are in the group?"

"Four regulars," Jessica said, then grinned. "Counting you and uncounting Bea. And we're more than a club. The other ladies are like my sisters, but we don't squabble as much." She glanced at her watch. "I've got to get back. According to Oliver, we may be in for some rocky times around here." She turned and headed for the door.

"Oliver?" Kaylee asked.

Mary sighed. "Oliver is a lavender geranium that 'tells the future.'"

Kaylee blinked, unsure how to respond.

Jessica halted and narrowed her eyes at Mary. "You mock, but Oliver predicted last year's storm and my first gray hair."

"How did he do that?" Kaylee asked, curiosity getting the best of her.

Mary rolled her eyes. "Jess is convinced that whenever Oliver's leaves are droopy or he loses too many petals at once, it's a bad omen." She leaned in and whispered loudly enough for Jessica to hear. "Our Jess can always be counted on for a good conspiracy theory. I think it stems from her empty-nest syndrome."

"I heard that," Jessica called over her shoulder. "I don't have time to argue now, but I shall remember the slight and we'll take it up later—over something chocolate." She reached for the door handle.

But before she could grab it, the door opened, exploding inward as a woman with blond hair and wild eyes rushed in, nearly knocking Jessica over. "He's coming! I can't believe it! He's coming!"

# 3

$B$ear scuttled behind the counter, watching the excited woman from his safe hiding place with uncertain eyes.

Mary's cheeks flushed red as her hands flew to her heart. "You're sure?"

The blond woman laughed a trifle hysterically. "I just got the e-mail from Ward Meacham's assistant confirming his participation in the book signing."

"Oh, DeeDee!" Mary rushed forward and gave her a hug. "This is so exciting! He hasn't been back to Orcas since *Never Too Bad* came out."

"So we'll actually get to meet him?" Jessica asked. "Get his signature? Shake his hand?"

The woman Mary had called DeeDee did a little happy dance. "I can't guarantee the handshake, but yes to the other two."

"*Never Too Bad*?" Even after years of being locked in her academic cocoon, Kaylee recognized the title and the author, though she'd never read the book. The way the women reacted, it was akin to Stephen King or John Grisham dropping in, not that she'd read them either.

"Unbelievable, right?" Mary looked like a starry-eyed teen about to meet her favorite rock star.

"He used to visit the island every year," DeeDee said. "There's this writers' group that comes here annually and stays for a week or two. A couple of them like Lorelei Lewis stay a month. They call themselves the Writers Coterie. Before Meacham hit it big, he came regularly as part of the group."

Kaylee frowned in thought. "Why do I know about the

Writers Coterie?" She mentally sifted through her academic contacts, especially those in the Lit Department. Nothing clicked.

"I don't know, but I have to tell you Meacham's visit is a shot in my financial arm." DeeDee did her happy dance again. "Like every other bookstore, Between the Lines has taken a beating from electronic books, but—"

"But you can't get an autograph on an electronic book," Mary finished for her. "And people still like autographs and celebrities."

"Exactly!"

"Can I bring my old copy of *Never Too Bad*, or do I have to buy a new one?" Jessica asked, her expression serious.

"Bring the old, but buy his new title."

"Do I have to?"

"Don't whine. It's unattractive. And yes you do!"

Jessica smiled. "Works for me. By the way, this is Kaylee Bleu."

DeeDee approached and shook Kaylee's hand. "I'm DeeDee Wilcox, and I'm a bit unhinged at the moment. Ward Meacham coming is the biggest thing to happen to Between the Lines since I bought the business. It means the whole island will be in my shop."

"I bet off-island people will make the trip too." Jessica hugged her flowers. "They're sure to need coffee, right?"

DeeDee's eyes widened at the thought. "Lots of coffee. Lots. There will be five other authors doing signings besides Ward."

"The regulars?" Mary asked without much enthusiasm.

"Three of them have new titles, including Lorelei Lewis."

Mary wrinkled her nose. "Lorelei's old-fashioned purple prose gives me toothaches." She rubbed her jaw as if she felt the pain.

"Yeah, but John Paul Jenkins's mysteries aren't too bad." DeeDee sounded like she was trying to convince a reluctant customer.

"No, they aren't bad," Jessica agreed, "even if I always know the killer by chapter two."

"Fortunately for him, not everyone's as clever as you."

Kaylee frowned. "I never read either writer, but I've seen Lorelei Lewis's book on paperback racks everywhere."

"She's relatively well-known," DeeDee said. "And if you're a mystery reader, you know John Paul Jenkins." She gave a little bounce. "But Ward Meacham! Class all the way. He'll put Between the Lines on the map."

"He is going to give all of us a day to remember for lots of reasons." Jessica rubbed her thumb and two fingers together. "Most of them crinkly, green, and numbered."

Kaylee bit back a laugh. She liked these women already.

"I've got so much to do!" DeeDee ran a hand through her hair as reality cut through her excitement. "It's already Monday and the signing's Saturday morning."

"What can we do to help?" Jessica asked. "Just tell us what you need."

"Absolutely," Mary agreed.

"I'm in too—if you'd like my help." Kaylee didn't want to force herself where she wasn't wanted.

DeeDee grabbed her in a hug. "I knew I was going to like you."

Mary looked at Kaylee. "Bea will still be here on the weekend for the signing, won't she? I think she knows Ward Meacham."

"She does? I'm surprised she knows someone that famous and has never mentioned it." *Ward Meacham.* Something elusive continued to float just out of mental reach. "I'll tell her he's coming when I get to the house."

"And I really do have to get back to Death by Chocolate," Jessica said, making a second attempt to get out the door. "See you tomorrow night at the lighthouse. We'll plan for the big event." With a wave, she left.

"See you then." DeeDee caught the door, ready to leave too. She paused and grinned at Kaylee. "Welcome to Orcas. It's not usually such a madhouse. Be sure and come with Bea to the meeting."

"I will." Kaylee wouldn't miss it for the world. She grinned at Mary as the door slipped closed behind DeeDee. "I'm going to like it here. I can tell."

"Of course you will." Mary walked back to the counter in the suddenly quiet shop.

"And we're going to like having you, especially here at the shop."

Bear peeked out from behind the counter as though trying to decide if it was safe to emerge. After a moment, he trotted over to Kaylee.

"Hey, handsome." She bent down and gave him a scratch down his back.

"Bea tells me you have her artistic eye for arranging." Mary leaned against the counter.

Kaylee chuckled. "She's very optimistic, especially where I'm concerned." She looked around the shop—*her* shop. Bea had removed many of the interior walls to create an open space that allowed comfortable movement between the gift items, the decorator pieces, and the largest area dedicated to everything fresh and floral with a heavy bridal touch. She remembered that the first floor was the retail shop, while the design studio and office were on the second floor, and the third floor was extra storage.

The sudden uncertainty she felt must have shone on her face because Mary said, "I'm sure you'll get the hang of it in no time."

Such encouragement spoken with great confidence was reassuring, even if Kaylee didn't entirely believe it.

"We do a surprising amount of business for such a small town and a small island," Mary continued. "Turtle Cove has become a popular wedding destination. Several of the local B&Bs specialize in marital bliss, and Bea works well with all of them." She smiled at Kaylee over her glasses. "Seeing you will be such a tonic for her."

Kaylee felt a jolt of alarm. "Has she been unwell?"

"Not ill, no. But she kind of lost her way when Ed disappeared. Her spark dimmed. They were the perfect couple, you know."

Kaylee knew. The firm foundation of her childhood visits had always been the affection between her grandparents. She'd sensed it even though as a child she couldn't have explained it.

"If only Bea knew what really happened . . ." Mary's voice held a deep sadness for her friend and employer.

The fact that no one knew what had happened to her grandfather haunted Kaylee, so she could only imagine how her grandmother must feel. People speculated, but that was the best anyone could do.

"I'd like to know more about that day," Kaylee said. "I've asked my grandmother, but—"

"I saw him that day."

"What?" Kaylee spun to see a woman dressed in a worn corduroy jacket and baggy jeans standing just inside the door. Her graying hair was windblown and cut at home, if Kaylee had to guess. A grumpy expression marred her features.

"I said I saw Ed Lyons that day. Watched him leave the marina."

"Roz Corzo! How come you never mentioned that before?" Mary glared, hands on her hips. In an aside to Kaylee she muttered, "Roz owns Corzo Whale Watch, and her boats are moored down at the marina by the ferry slip."

"Who says I never mentioned it before?" Roz glared right back. "I told the people who mattered, like the police."

Mary didn't back down. "Did you tell Bea?"

"It's none of your business if I did or I didn't."

"You didn't. Roz, how could you? It might have helped her."

"How would telling her that Ed left the marina wearing that floppy hat he always wore to keep the sun off his bald head help? She already knew that."

"I remember that hat." Kaylee narrowed her eyes. "Even when I was a kid, he was going bald and wore it. I don't remember the brand name, but it had a lifetime guarantee. He'd already worn out two by the time I was twenty. He'd send in the worn-out one, and a week or so later a new one would show up at no expense."

"Just who are you?" Roz demanded. "You're not thinking of moving here, are you?"

"Actually—"

"Where are you from? California?"

Kaylee blinked at the woman's harsh tone. Clearly California was bad. "No."

"Good. We got too many Californians moving up here and ruining things." Roz's scowl deepened. "They take it personal that they have to live by the ferry schedule, and the grocery don't have all the fancy and weird veggies and stuff they got down there, and the organic nonsense it has isn't organic enough for them. Complain, complain, complain. It's bad enough when they're just tourists, but when they move here . . ."

She continued as Kaylee began to worry about her blood pressure. "This very morning I took a party of six Californians on a private whale-watching excursion in the Zodiak. All they could do was gripe. It was too cold. It was too windy. It was too rough. They were getting wet. What did they expect in a small boat on open water? Makes me sick."

Mary held up her hand. "Easy, Roz."

Roz snorted. "Tell me this. Is it my fault the orcas decided to hide today?"

Kaylee remembered going whale watching as a kid and not seeing a single whale. It had been disappointing, but she couldn't blame the guide. "I'm sorry you had such a bad trip."

"No. Good trip, but we didn't find them until the last twenty minutes even with all that electronic stuff we use these days. What's their gripe? We found 'em. They were waking from their naps, breeching, playing. It was a great show."

"I'd have loved to see it." Kaylee smiled.

Roz squinted at her. "Who did you say you were?"

Mary answered the question. "This is Kaylee Bleu, Bea's granddaughter. She's taking over The Flower Patch from Bea."

"Huh." Roz studied Kaylee with a definite lack of pleasure. "So you *are* moving here."

The local Chamber of Commerce should never put Roz on the welcoming committee. "I am, but not from California. Just from Seattle. Bear and I are excited about living on Orcas."

"Wait until you miss the ferry. Then see how excited you are. And who's Bear?"

Hearing his name, Bear stopped exploring the store and came scrabbling toward Roz.

Roz jumped back, then scowled down at the dog. "Is that one of them ridiculous city purse dogs?"

"Bear is not a purse dog." Kaylee tried not to laugh at what Bear would undoubtedly think of as defamation of character. It was obvious he thought he was a mighty Saint Bernard in disguise, keeping the world safe for democracy. Or on days like today when he wore one of his bow ties, he was a magazine cover model.

Roz grunted as she studied the little dog who studied her right back. "I gotta get back to the boat. Just thought I'd duck in here a minute and look at the flowers. They usually cheer me up, and I need cheering up after those Californians."

"Well, you come back and look at them anytime," Mary said. "I want a fistful of mixed carnations for my office. They last a long time. I can look at them and save myself the trip here."

Kaylee walked to the cooler and retrieved several colorful *Dianthus caryophyllus* and a couple of *Rumohra adiantiformis*. She arranged the leatherleaf fern with the yellow, pink, rose, and cream carnations. "How's this?" She held the flowers out to Roz, who eyed them critically before she gave a nod.

Mary held out her hand. "Allow me." She took the flowers and wrapped them in green florist's tissue and tied a small pink ribbon to hold the paper closed.

Roz paid Mary, cradled the flowers in the crook of her arm, and walked to the door. She paused and looked at Kaylee, then down at Bear who returned her gaze with bright eyes. "He's sorta cute, but he looks kinda like one of the rats down at the dock, doesn't he?" Bear responded with a single, sharp bark, and Roz left.

Kaylee stared after Roz. "Now there is one interesting woman."

Mary laughed. "On an island that loves quirky, Roz is in a class by herself."

"Is she always that grumpy? She seems so unhappy." Especially when contrasted with Mary, Jessica, and DeeDee, the other women she'd met today.

"I've known Roz all her life. She's never been a particularly glass-half-full kind of person, but she's become increasingly bitter and negative since her husband died. Richard was dedicated to her. Made her laugh. When he passed, she was devastated. She's managed to hold the business together. But herself? Not so much."

"Sad."

"Very. I took the call the night he died." Mary shook her head. "That was a bad night."

Kaylee looked at her quizzically.

"I was the police dispatcher for years."

"Really? That must have been an interesting job."

"That's a good word for it, but I always say between me and Herb—that's my husband—he had the more dangerous job."

"What was he? A police officer?"

"A mail carrier. He drove the whole island every day. He ran into all kinds of situations. He's retired now like me and volunteers with the Youth Association to keep himself and the kids out of trouble." Mary grinned mischievously as she looked over Kaylee's shoulder. "Speaking of trouble."

Kaylee turned as the door opened and in walked a tall, muscular man wearing a black T-shirt with a red and black plaid flannel shirt thrown over it as a makeshift jacket. He had sandy hair and a light scruff that might be the beginnings of an intentional beard, or the result of being too busy to shave. He smiled at Mary and then Kaylee, whose heart—usually very nonverbal—went "Whoa!"

"What can I do for you, Reese?" Mary asked.

Kaylee filed away that name in her mind.

"I want to get some flowers for Mrs. Murphy," he said. "She wasn't feeling too well when I was fixing her porch railing, and I thought a small bouquet of something colorful might cheer her up."

*He sends flowers to sick old ladies? Double whoa!*

"That's so nice of you." Mary grinned and gestured to Kaylee. "This is Kaylee Bleu, Bea's granddaughter and my new boss. Kaylee, this is Reese Holt, master carpenter and the island's premier handyman."

Reese offered his hand. "Hi, Kaylee. I heard you were coming. Bea has talked of nothing else."

As Kaylee shook his hand, she tried to ignore the zing she felt when his calloused palm touched hers. Granted he was a good-looking guy—a *very* good-looking guy—but the zing was ridiculous. She might not have had much of a dating life recently, workaholic that she was, but even she knew "zings" were for high school kids and first loves, not mature women starting second careers.

Bear darted behind her, drawing her attention from Reese before she embarrassed herself. The little dog was clearly nervous of Reese's big work boots. He offered a single bark, half greeting and half uncertainty.

Reese grinned down at Bear. "That's one fierce dog you've got there."

"This is Bear, my best buddy and protector."

"Bear? Cute name for someone barely there." Reese crouched. "How you doing, big guy?" He held out his hand.

Bear edged out from behind Kaylee and sniffed. He looked up at her, checking before he stuck his head under Reese's hand for a scratch. If he'd been a cat, he'd have been purring in about three seconds.

Reese stood, and Bear pouted as his new friend turned his attention to Kaylee. "Are you heading out to Wildflower Cottage?"

"I am."

"I'm going that way too. I promised your grandmother I'd be out to check a squeaky floorboard and anything else that needs fixing. She wants the place perfect for you."

Kaylee felt warmed through, though whether at Bea's care for her or Reese's handsome smile she wasn't certain.

"If you don't mind me crashing your reunion," he continued, "I'll follow my original plan to fix that floorboard and whatever else I find."

Kaylee hoped she didn't look as pleased as she felt. "That sounds good."

Reese paid for the flowers he'd ordered and left the shop.

Mary slid the register drawer closed. "Most eligible bachelor on the island."

"I can believe it." Kaylee watched Reese disappear from view, then turned to find Mary grinning at her.

"You couldn't do better," Mary said.

Kaylee felt her face flame. "No matchmaking please. I haven't even unpacked yet. Let me at least get settled."

Mary held her hands up. "Of course. That's all I want. To get everyone . . . settled."

With a laugh and a wave, Kaylee left the shop. The drive to Wildflower Cottage passed quickly. She reveled in the green of the conifers, the pink spikes of the *Digitalis purpurea,* vibrant reds of the *Castilleja linariaefolia,* and the soft purple of *Lavandula.* Make that foxglove, Indian paintbrush, and lavender. She'd have to get used to using the common names of flowers when helping customers at The Flower Patch.

When she rounded a curve and saw Wildflower Cottage, she felt her cares melting away. She'd loved the white, cottage-style farmhouse from the moment she'd first laid eyes on it as a child. The tall windows let in lots of sunlight to shine on the gleaming wood floors and comfortable furniture. As she pulled into the drive, she could see the field of lavender and wildflowers behind the house. She remembered the peace of evenings spent sitting on the back deck as the sun set, her grandparents talking about their day as she enjoyed an ice-cream cone. To this day, the scent of lavender made her happy.

As Kaylee's tires crunched on the gravel and she parked beside Reese's black truck, Beatrice Lyons stepped onto the porch, waving her welcome. She was a small woman with hazel eyes and curly gray hair. Her reading glasses hung on a colorful chain about her neck, where she kept them so they wouldn't get lost. They often got lost anyway, and many of her phone calls to Kaylee were full of funny stories about where they finally showed up.

Kaylee released Bear from his seat belt, tucked him under her arm, and hurried up the steps to greet her grandmother. The two hugged, sandwiching the little dog between them and making him bark with excitement.

Kaylee took a step backward and put Bear down. "Go run around a bit, buddy." He gave a happy yip and spun in excited circles. Kaylee laughed at him and looked at Bea. "Poor boy's been cooped up all day. He'll calm down soon."

"Then he'll be doing better than me. I'm so excited to have you here!"

Kaylee hugged her grandmother again. Why hadn't she visited more? "I'm glad to be here too."

"It makes me so happy to know that you're taking over."

"I'll take good care of everything. I promise."

Bea took Kaylee's hand and pulled her into the house. "I know you will. And I'm getting it all fixed up for you."

Kaylee heard the screech of a board complaining about being moved. "I met Reese at the shop. He said he was coming here."

Bea grinned. "If my heart didn't still belong to Ed . . ."

Kaylee laughed. "Grandma!" she said as if scandalized.

"Bea? You should come see this." Reese's strained voice drew them to the front guest room, which had been Ed's study. Reese knelt on the floor by Ed's desk. A piece of unattached floorboard lay beside him. Bear rushed over to stick his nose in the dark hole in the floor, his tail wagging madly.

"Don't tell me you found a mouse," Bea said. "I thought I won the mouse wars."

"No one on the island wins the mouse wars. You know that. But this is no mouse." He reached down and lifted a leather-bound book from the space below the board. "Someone used this space as a hidey-hole."

Hand over her mouth, Bea walked over and took the book. She flipped gently through the pages, then hugged it to her.

Kaylee looked over Bea's shoulder. "What is it?" But she thought she knew. She glanced at the bookcase that lined the far wall. Similar books filled one whole shelf.

"It's one of Ed's journals." Bea's smile grew wistful. "I always bought him one for his birthday. It was a joke that I looked for ones that were attractive, but no flowers allowed. Flowers were too girlie. It had to be masculine. We used to argue over what was manly enough that he wouldn't be ashamed to be caught writing in it." She sighed. "Oh, Ed, why'd you hide it in the floor?"

Kaylee glanced at Reese, and he looked as unable to answer as she felt.

"He wrote everything down." Bea smiled as tears welled in her eyes at the memory. "Everything. Remember, Kaylee? Books he read, plants or animals he spotted, places we went, ideas he wanted to explore. He was forever looking things up in his journals to settle arguments about when we did such and such. He won every single argument." She let out another sigh and glanced at the shelf of journals. "I used to threaten to burn them all. Of course we both knew I never would."

Kaylee studied the volume in her grandmother's hands. "Maybe he wrote down something he wanted to keep secret."

"From me?" Bea looked hurt at the mere suggestion.

"Not *from* you." Kaylee made haste to explain. "Maybe about something he was planning to do *for* you. A surprise, like a trip or a party or something." She couldn't imagine her beloved grandfather doing anything bad that he would have to hide.

Bea stood quietly, eyes closed, once again hugging the book close. Then she held it out to Kaylee. "You take it. You can tell me if there's anything in it I need to know."

"Are you sure?" Kaylee was afraid her mentioning a possible secret had made her grandmother leery about reading it.

"It's too painful, you know. It's like when I couldn't stand to look at my favorite picture of the two of us for a couple of years after he died because it wasn't the two of us anymore."

Kaylee's heart hurt at her grandmother's pain. "I'd be honored to read the journal for you."

Bea gave a little snort, morphing back into the gutsy woman Kaylee so admired. "You probably won't thank me. Ed had the worst handwriting."

"You forget. I've been reading the scribblings of professors for years, to say nothing of the occasional note from a student that didn't come off a computer."

"Then you're just the person for this job." Bea turned to Reese. "Can you put the board back so it won't squeak?"

"Sure. Ed merely tacked it in place so he could have easy access. I'll nail it firmly. No problem."

"Thanks, Reese. I hope when you're finished, you'll have time to enjoy a piece of pie."

"Your famous apple amber?"

"You bet. It's my bow to my Irish ancestry." She gave a little bend at the waist.

"My favorite."

Bea looked back and forth between Reese and Kaylee. "Something you two have in common."

Kaylee nearly laughed out loud. *Real subtle, Grandma.*

"Mmm," Reese said. Whether in response to the pie or Bea's comment, Kaylee didn't know.

It was several hours before she had a chance to open the journal. Wearing her favorite pajamas with images of multicolored dachshunds running all over them, she settled in the big bed in the guest room. She flipped the journal open to the last page to read her grandfather's final written words.

What she saw on the page made her gasp. With trembling hands, she read and reread the words, their unequivocal implications sending chills up her spine:

*Tomorrow I'm heading out to learn the truth. I must be careful, as I'm afraid I've already made the killer suspicious. If I don't come back, my darling Bea, know this: It was no accident. It was murder.*

# 4

Kaylee stared at the words in Ed's loopy, sloppy cursive. Murder only happened on TV shows and in the news. It only happened to people you didn't know, people you didn't love. Certainly not to one of the most important men in your life. Murders happened in Los Angeles, Chicago, maybe even Seattle. But in Turtle Cove?

If her own heart was pounding with outrage and distress, what would such a possibility do to her grandmother?

And what had Ed learned that would put his life in danger? He was a kind and caring man. How did he get involved with someone capable of homicide? If he had indeed been murdered, it wasn't a random crime where he was in the wrong place at the wrong time. There was foreknowledge here.

She leafed backward through the journal, looking for more information.

*I cannot believe what I have discovered.* That was the first mention of whatever he had learned, written about a week before his death.

*I have checked the evidence three or four times, and it always comes out the same—criminal and deliberate. I don't want it to be this way.* What way? And what evidence? Kaylee felt frustrated at the general nature of the comments. How could they ever find out the guilty party if Ed didn't name names or state specifics?

*What should I do? I can't undo what's been done, but does it go beyond theft?* Did what go beyond theft? Theft of what?

Kaylee closed her eyes and took a deep breath to calm herself, but it didn't work. She felt chilled all over, and the hair on her arms stood at attention. She attacked the journal, desperate for more information. As she read back through the book, it was full of ordinary things—dinners out with his wife, friends coming over, discussions of the national news with pungent remarks about a couple of friends with whom he strongly disagreed, the progress of his garden, the new wedding contracts Bea got, his reactions to books he read, the anticipation of a visit from Kaylee's parents.

A couple of days before he disappeared, he mentioned Kaylee herself, and her heart jumped.

*I read about this fascinating and rare flower that's been found over on Deception Island. I want to go over and check it out. I can't wait to tell Kaylee about it. I'll send her pictures. Maybe we can finally get her out here again.*

Kaylee stared at the words for a long time, her eyes filling with tears. I'd have come, Grandpa. But would she have? She had been so caught up in her work at the university and with the police that she'd probably have settled for the pictures. Of course if she'd known . . .

It was a few minutes before she took a deep breath and began reading again.

*I cannot believe what I have discovered.*

And no indication what it was that he'd discovered. The flower? Had he gone to Deception Island? But why would a flower lead to his death? And what would cause an experienced boater to disappear on a day when the weather was calm and the water as smooth and unruffled as a tabletop? Or had he discovered something totally unrelated to the flower?

Kaylee rubbed her arms to ease the chill, but it came from inside. What should she do with this information? Certainly she should tell the police, but what could they do? Everything was so vague!

And what could she tell Bea? "Sorry to ruin your life when you're starting a new chapter in Arizona, but Grandpa was murdered." No, she couldn't.

Frustrated and forlorn, she got out of bed and tiptoed to the hall. A strip of light showed under Bea's door. Not a surprise. She'd always been a night owl. It was a family joke that she and Grandpa passed each other as she went to bed and he rose.

Kaylee stared at the strip of light. She should wait until morning to say something. Such terrible news was better learned in the sunshine after a good night's sleep.

Her grandmother's bedroom door opened as Kaylee stood shivering in the hall, hugging the journal.

"Oh!" Bea jumped when she saw Kaylee, her hand going to her heart. "You startled me. What are you doing skulking out here? Are you hungry too? Want another piece of that pie? And get a robe. It's chilly."

Bea continued to the kitchen without waiting for answers to her questions. Kaylee returned to her room, grabbed a robe, and followed her grandmother, still unsure how to pass on the information she had learned.

When Bea paused with a knife over the bit of pie that still remained, she turned to Kaylee. "How big?"

"Little." Kaylee held her thumb and forefinger close together. The way her stomach clenched, she doubted she could eat even that amount.

"Is that Ed's journal you're clutching?"

Kaylee nodded.

Bea studied her. "You found something bad." She collapsed in a chair at the table, pie forgotten, her face a mask of distress. "There *are* secrets he kept from me."

Kaylee sank into the chair across from her grandmother. "No, no, no!" She grabbed her grandmother's hand. "Nothing like you're worried about. He calls you his darling Bea."

"He does?" Tears filled Bea's eyes.

"Of course he does. Believe me."

Bea's tears overflowed and suddenly she was sobbing.

"Grandma!"

Kaylee wasn't sure what to do at this unexpected turn of events, but hugs always worked. She rounded the table, grabbed her grandmother, and held on.

The tears eventually lessened and Bea sniffed. She pulled from Kaylee's embrace. "Darling Bea? Really?"

"Really. He adored you." Kaylee didn't offer to show Bea in the journal—the murder part might send her into another crying jag.

"What a relief! He didn't leave with some young chick or go live with a second family he chose over me."

"Of course he didn't." Had she been worrying about something like that for five years?

Bea shrugged. "I watch a lot of movies and read a lot of novels. I have a vivid imagination."

"He loved you and only you, darling Bea."

Her smile was brilliant. "He always called me that when I exasperated him. 'Darling Bea,' he'd say, 'how can you be so wrong and so wonderful at the same time?' I know he loved me, I do, but still it's wonderful to hear."

She slapped her knees in a return to gutsy Bea and started to rise. "Let me get you that pie." Then she studied Kaylee's face and sat again. "There's more, isn't there? Go ahead. Tell me. I can take it. It can't be worse than all these years of not knowing what happened."

Kaylee took a deep breath and blurted, "He might have been murdered."

"Murdered!" Bea grabbed the table to steady herself.

"He discovered something bad about someone."

"Who and what?"

Kaylee shook her head. "He doesn't name names or state specifics. Just general comments like *I cannot believe what I discovered.*"

Bea grabbed the book from Kaylee. "Where?"

"The last few pages."

Kaylee stared at her grandmother's bowed head and waited.

"Why didn't he tell me?" Bea looked at Kaylee as if she expected an answer. "We could have faced the problem together."

Kaylee's heart caught at the sorrow and regret on her grandmother's face. "Maybe he thought he was keeping you safe. He was protecting you."

Bea gave an unladylike snort. "That would be just like him, the old fool." She got slowly to her feet and, journal in hand, walked to her bedroom and closed the door, leaving Kaylee, without an appetite, staring at the uneaten pie.

# 5

"I think you should put your authors in the back of the store for the signing." Jessica put her coffee cup down on the table in the lightkeeper's quarters at the Old Cape Lighthouse. "Make the customers walk through your stock and get the idea they want more than Ward Meacham's signature."

"I usually put them near the front." DeeDee looked thoughtful. "You know. Draw the people in."

"Sure, when you weren't sure people would bother walking to the back for your authors. But with Ward coming . . ."

Mary laughed. "Don't tell Lorelei Lewis she wouldn't draw her fans to the back of the store."

"If any of her fans come, they'll find her no matter where she is in the store. They're rabid."

The five women of the Petal Pushers sat around the table at the Old Cape Lighthouse planning for the Saturday morning book signing.

"I'll supply not only a selection of chocolate goodies, but little quiches and, of course, quality coffees and teas." Jessica made notes in her phone.

"We'll do a cheese board." Bea looked at Kaylee, who nodded. "And, of course, flowers as needed."

"Food and I don't do well together." Mary laughed at herself. "Just ask my husband. I'll contribute a free morning's labor. I'll work the register so you can mingle with your customers."

"You guys are the greatest, but—" DeeDee held up her index finger "—make sure you give me your bills for services rendered."

"But of course," Bea said. "All this is strictly business. We're using you for free advertising."

Kaylee looked at the women and had to smile despite spending all day worrying about Ed's journal and all it portended. DeeDee wasn't going to get any bills.

Mary, Jessica, and DeeDee continued talking, clarifying the arrangement of tables and chairs for the signing, the position of the various writers at the table so no one's feelings would be hurt, and where the refreshments should be set up.

"I have a list of specifics for Ward." DeeDee looked more than slightly grumpy. "His assistant sent them. He needs a pitcher of chilled bottled water, brand specified, and a glass, the water to be replaced when it warms."

"He can't just have the bottle and chug it like everyone else?" Jessica looked equally miffed.

"Apparently not. He needs five black markers. Not four, not six, five. He needs at least one hundred copies of his new title as well as several of his old ones."

"One hundred?" Jessica looked surprised. "This is Orcas, not Seattle. We don't have crowds of thousands wandering around, even for famous people."

"One hundred books. And he needs a comfortable chair. I ask you, do they think I'll put him in an uncomfortable one? *And* I have to have someone at the ferry to lead them here."

Jessica laughed. "I don't think they could get lost between the ferry and Turtle Cove if they tried. Besides, Ward used to come here all the time when he was part of the Writers Coterie. He'd rent the old Mermaid Cottage over near Eastsound."

"In fairness," DeeDee said, "those requests didn't come from him."

Mary looked relieved. "He was never above himself back in the days before he was famous, was he, Bea?"

Bea looked up from studying her clasped hands resting in her lap. "I'm sorry. Could you repeat that? Who wasn't what?"

Mary sat back in her chair and looked from Bea to Kaylee and back. "Okay, give. What's bothering you two? You've barely been here all evening. Is the transition of The Flower Patch not going as planned?"

Bea waved a hand, flicking away any such suggestion. "No, everything's fine there." Her emphasis on *there* made it obvious things weren't fine elsewhere.

Mary, Jessica, and DeeDee continued studying Bea and Kaylee, waiting.

Kaylee bit her lip. These women were her grandmother's friends, so it was up to Bea to decide what to tell them.

With a sigh Bea bent to her big purse resting on the floor beside her. She pulled out a sheaf of papers, and Kaylee could see Ed's loopy writing on the pages.

"Here." She passed sheets to each of the women. "I made copies for you. They're from one of Ed's journals."

Silence filled the room as the women read. Then questions exploded.

"Discovery? What discovery?" DeeDee looked confused.

"Murder? Is he kidding?" Jessica looked appalled.

"Murder would explain a lot," Mary said.

"That's it? That's all he wrote?" Jessica flipped the papers front to back. "Where's the rest?"

Bea shrugged. "That's all there is."

"No!" Jessica wailed. "Not fair."

"And you just found it?" Mary asked.

"Reese found Ed's journal while he was doing some repairs." Bea spread her copy of the journal on the table, running her hand back and forth over the words as if through them she could touch her husband.

"Hidden?" Mary pushed her glasses back on her nose.

"Under a floorboard."

The women looked suitably concerned. "Gosh, Bea," Mary finally said. "What are you going to do?"

"Did you call the police?" Jessica asked. "You should if you haven't already."

"We called this morning," Kaylee said. "They have the journal, but we made copies before they got to the house."

"But what can they do with only this?" DeeDee held out her pages. "There's no name, no nothing."

"Exactly," Bea said.

Silence fell again as they all considered that reality.

"Bea, I'm so sorry." DeeDee leaned forward, her face earnest. "Here I am fussing about the signing, and you have a real problem. Ed possibly murdered!"

"It's something I hate to even consider." Bea patted DeeDee's hand. "But that doesn't mean the signing isn't important too. It is, and I'm glad I have something to think about while the police do whatever they manage to do."

The door to the room flew open, cool air rushed in, and there stood a woman of substance in all definitions of the phrase. Tall, titian-haired, buxom, and self-assured, she posed for a second in the doorway.

She was greeted by a moment of stunned surprise as she smiled with regal condescension.

"Lorelei!" DeeDee finally managed. "We didn't expect you tonight."

*Lorelei Lewis?* Kaylee gaped.

It must have been. The newcomer nodded with queenly grace, royalty to a lesser mortal.

"Don't tell her," Bea hissed to the Petals as she slid her copy of the journal pages into her purse. Kaylee watched as all the

Petals somehow made their pages disappear as Lorelei turned to shut the door.

"I knew it was you girls." Lorelei took possession of the room as if they had all been waiting with great expectation for her. "I just had to stop and say hello. It is so good to be back!"

On a wave of fragrance and bonhomie, Lorelei went around the table dispensing hugs and kisses until she came to Kaylee. "You're new." She threw an accusatory glare around the group. "She's new. I thought Petal Pushers was a closed society. You never asked me to join." Unspoken was the clear idea that it was their loss.

Bea ignored Lorelei's sniping and beamed at Kaylee. "She's my granddaughter, Katherine Leigh Bleu, called Kaylee because Ed said her given name was too big for a little bitty thing like her. Of course she was about five hours old when he said it."

"Not so little now," Kaylee said with a wry smile.

Bea grinned. "But the name stuck. She's taking over The Flower Patch and Wildflower Cottage."

Lorelei turned her intent gaze on Bea. "You planning to die or something and picked your successor ahead of time?"

Bea snorted. "I'm moving to Arizona."

Lorelei grabbed an empty chair and lowered herself dramatically into it. "Arizona? What's it got but cacti and heat?"

"My twin sister lives there. I'm moving in with her."

"These ladies don't argue with you enough?" She jerked her head at the other Petals. "You have to revert to your childhood and your sisterly contentions?"

"My sister and I never argue." Bea looked offended.

"Of course not."

"Well, not much. I don't like to argue."

"Too bad Ed's not here to tell us the truth." Lorelei sighed and put a hand tipped with long, shiny red nails over her heart. "What a wonderful man."

"My husband certainly was wonderful." Bea glanced at Kaylee. "You're scaring my granddaughter. She's never seen anyone like Lorelei Lewis, romance writer."

Lorelei laughed and turned to Kaylee. "It is a bit overwhelming when I assume my flamboyant author persona, isn't it?" She smiled and gone was her dramatic manner. In its place was a pleasant, middle-aged woman, someone you'd meet in the grocery store and gossip with over your shopping carts. She stuck out her hand. "Lorie Loblinski, a.k.a. Lorelei Lewis. Glad to meet you."

Blinking at the transformation, Kaylee automatically shook Lorie's hand.

Lorie studied Kaylee. "You know, Bea, she would make an excellent heroine. Beautiful face, all that dark hair, and those wonderful green eyes."

"You are not to put her in one of your sordid stories, Lorie."

"Don't worry, Bea. No one will recognize her by the time I get finished with her." Lorie winked at Kaylee, and Kaylee had to laugh at the mischievous twinkle in Lorie's eye.

"And, girls, have I got news for you. So sad." Lorie put her hand over her mouth. "I'm trying to hold in my smile. I don't want to seem too catty." But it was clear she couldn't wait to spill whatever it was she knew.

"Okay, give," Bea said cooperatively.

"Right." Lorie paused for effect, then leaned in like she was imparting a great secret. Kaylee found herself leaning in too. "Word on the street is that Ward has received no interest in his latest book for a film. None. Zip. Zero." She slapped her hand over her mouth again. "I've got to stop smiling when I say that, but isn't it a shame? Oh, drat, I'm smiling again, aren't I?"

"Lorie, you're shameless." But DeeDee was smiling too.

"Lorelei's never had one of her books made into a movie," Bea whispered to Kaylee.

"I figured," Kaylee whispered back.

"I heard that," Lorie said. "Hallmark almost came through once. But that's beside the point. I'm talking golden boy Ward."

DeeDee reached for one of Jessica's double chocolate brownies. "I do know the reviews of *On Ice* have not been all that positive."

"They've been terrible!" Lorie grabbed a brownie too and put it on the napkin she filched. "You should see the ones online. Brutal." She pressed her lips together. "I'm not smiling, am I?"

DeeDee studied Lorie. "I thought you liked Ward."

"I used to. He used to be nice. He used to remember he had friends. He used to sit for hours brainstorming plot and talking characters. He used to encourage all of us in the Writers Coterie, even when we had more success than he. Now he makes believe he never knew us. We gave him all the help we could when he released *Never Too Late* as a complete unknown. Then boom! Fame followed by memory loss." She bit into her brownie as if it had offended her, not Ward.

"I guess you haven't heard," DeeDee said. "He's coming Saturday for the signing."

Lorie looked bowled over. "You're kidding! He's actually coming to Orcas?"

"I got the word today."

Lorie rubbed her forehead as if she had a headache. "Now I feel the fool. He's coming to the Coterie. I'm going to have to be nice and learn to like him again." She sighed and stood. "I have to go back to the Turtle Cove Inn and work on my 'nice to have you back' speech. I hope I have the acting chops to pull it off." And she left, taking her extraordinary energy and charisma with her. The room seemed flat when she disappeared into the encroaching dusk.

It was quiet for a minute as the Petals all regrouped like dazed citizens after the victorious army had withdrawn, the celebrations were over, and only the rebuilding remained. Then DeeDee spoke up. "I don't want to be around when she finds out he's not staying for the Coterie."

# 6

Kaylee was working at the weathered desk in the office at The Flower Patch Wednesday afternoon when Mary stuck her head in. "Reese is here, and he's asking for you." Mary waggled her eyebrows significantly.

Kaylee ignored Mary's implicating eyebrows. "What's he want?"

"He didn't say, and I didn't ask. He just wants you."

Kaylee rolled her eyes. "Tell him I'll be right there."

Mary disappeared back downstairs to relay the message. Kaylee saved her work on the computer, stood, and wiped nervous palms down her jeans. Bear rose from his nap and watched her as she checked her appearance in the mirror on the bathroom door. She had her straight hair pulled back in a low ponytail so it wouldn't keep falling forward as she worked. Severe perhaps, but classic, emphasizing her cheekbones, a gift from her father's Native American ancestry. Too bad about the circles under her eyes, which were courtesy of Ed's journal and all the unruly thoughts it had unleashed, making sleep difficult, if not impossible.

Taking a deep breath, she went into the store, Bear padding at her side. Reese was leaning against the counter talking to Mary. He straightened and smiled when he saw her. Was she imagining appreciation in his eyes? Bear rushed to him, apparently accepting him as a best friend in the new neighborhood. Reese bent to say hello, then straightened.

"You have a minute, Kaylee?" He really did have a cute smile.

"Anytime." She flushed at how forward that sounded, but

what woman in her right mind wouldn't have a moment for him? "Let's get a cup of coffee at Jess's while we talk."

"Go ahead." Mary waved them out the door. "Bear and I will be fine here."

With a cup of English afternoon tea and a chocolate muffin that was still warm from the oven, Kaylee sat at one of the little tables in Death by Chocolate. She reached out and gently touched the vibrant pink *Gerbera jamesonii* in the vase in the center of the table. She couldn't help but smile.

"You look happy." Reese slid into the chair opposite.

She gave the daisy a final pat. "I still can't believe I'm living on Orcas."

"Academia's loss is our gain." Reese took a sip of his steaming coffee. "Ouch." He glanced over his shoulder at Jessica. "There's a difference between hot and scalding, you know. I think I'll have to file suit for both mental and physical cruelty."

Jessica smiled. "I'm so scared."

Kaylee took a bite of her muffin. She closed her eyes in appreciation.

"Jess has the touch." Reese took a forkful of his chocolate cheesecake. "So good." He paused before continuing. "Are you familiar with a writer named Porter Ashford? He wrote fantasy and used to live here on the island."

"Sure, I know Mr. Ashford. *One World Too Many. The Moon Is Down.* He was a good friend of my grandfather's, probably his best friend."

"Then you probably know that his children have been fighting over his estate ever since his death."

"Grandma mentioned it, but she didn't really go into details."

"Apparently the problem is Jules, the middle child. Or maybe I should say Jules's wife, Bettina. The other Ashfords, Isaac and Ursula, are very nice people, as are their spouses and kids."

"I used to play with Mr. Ashford's grandkids when we were little and they came to the island to visit their grandparents," Kaylee said. "How awful that his kids are fighting over this. What is it with families and that one child who drives everyone crazy?"

Reese sipped his coffee more cautiously this time. "Or who marries someone like Bettina who throws the family into chaos? You know how your grandma generally likes everyone? Bettina is a rare exception to that rule." Reese grinned. "According to Bea, Bettina is demanding and difficult and expects to be served. She thinks she's the only one who knows the right way to do things, and she has the gall to call Porter's writing his 'hobby.' But what really gets Bea's goat is that Bettina refuses to come to Orcas. Apparently she came here once, got mad at Ursula about some little thing, and announced she was leaving rather than be so disrespected. She was furious when she learned she had to wait until the ferry came the next morning. Ruined her dramatic exit."

Kaylee laughed. "If you're crazy enough not to like Orcas, the least you can do is keep your opinion to yourself."

"Bettina is not long on tact, I've heard. For some reason she's decided Jules is being cheated in the disposition of assets. It's all about the royalties from Porter's many books. Instead of having his will say all income should be divided equally between the three children, which would have been seen as equitable even to someone as blind as Bettina, he assigned certain titles and their royalties to each kid."

"And Bettina thinks Jules got books that make less money?" Kaylee was fascinated.

"Right. Jules got a fair share as far as number of books, but one of his titles is an unknown. No one, not even Porter's publisher, knows anything about that manuscript. They've never even seen it. So Jules and Bettina have contested every single legal pronouncement since Porter's death, starting with his will."

"That's crazy!" Kaylee protested. "Mr. Ashford died two years before my grandfather!"

Reese scraped up the last of his cheesecake and looked with longing at the remaining slices in the display cooler. He took a deep breath and turned from temptation. "At any rate, I guess they've finally settled things because I've been hired to fix up the house and grounds and get them ready for sale."

Kaylee tore off another piece of her muffin. "I always loved visiting Mr. Ashford with Grandpa when I was a kid, even if his grandkids weren't there. He was such a nice man. He always made me snow cones, those shaved ice things with flavored syrup. He had this old machine that spit out the shaved ice. He'd scoop up some and put it in a paper cup. Then I'd get to pick my flavor for the day. He had several flavors, but I always picked root beer. He used to set up a snow cone booth at community or church events, all profits going to whatever organization was running the event."

Reese looked thoughtful. "Didn't he write a kids' book about an evil snow cone machine that made everyone who ate its product into slaves and dullards until Prince Isaac came along and broke the evil spell and saved the day?"

"I remember sitting on Grandpa's lap while Mr. Ashford read the story to us," Kaylee said fondly.

"I don't remember a comparable book about Prince Jules," Reese said. "Maybe that's what soured Jules, and he's been getting even for the perceived slight for the past seven years."

"No, there is a Jules book and an Ursula book. In his, Jules gets to save the kingdom just like Isaac. In Ursula's, she gets to save the whole world as she and her singing dragon fly around righting wrongs, sort of a medieval superhero with her melodic sidekick. Mr. Ashford would never favor one of his children over another. He was a wonderful man—quiet, kind, fair."

"I wish I'd had a chance to know him." Reese put his crumpled napkin on his empty plate. He fiddled with the Los Angeles Dodgers baseball cap resting on the table beside him.

Kaylee looked at the well-worn cap, then pointed her finger at him. "You're one of those Californians Roz Corzo dislikes, aren't you?"

"Just because I like the Dodgers? Not even Roz would hold that against a person." He tipped his chair back on two legs. "And I repaired the whale watch dock and saved her from a huge fine not too long after her husband died, when she was trying to find a way to keep the business going. Now I'm one of her favorites." He puffed his chest, making Kaylee laugh.

"I bet you didn't charge her full price, did you?" She wasn't certain how she knew this, but she did. "You gave her your damsel-in-distress discount."

He shrugged. "I try to match my rates to what my clients can afford. For instance, I have no compunction about charging the Ashfords full fare for fixing up their place. That particular well is far from dry."

"Unless legal fees ate up everything—which would be awful. I'm glad Mr. Ashford doesn't know what's going on with the estate. He'd be devastated that his kids were fighting." Kaylee poured the last of her tea from the little yellow teapot into her flowered cup. "Mr. Ashford came to my grandparents' for dinner every Wednesday. His wife died when I was a little kid, and Grandma decided he should eat well at least one night a week. Those Wednesday night dinners lasted for years and years, probably until he died. I loved just sitting and listening to everyone. He always talked about his latest novel. I was fascinated by all the parallel universes and other worlds he created. Apparently others were too since he made a tidy fortune with his work."

"Didn't you say you've been to his house too?"

"Lots of times."

"That's great. Then you know what it should look like, what it looked like when Porter was alive. I'd love your help with fixing the place up."

"*My* help?" She laughed. "I don't think so. Hammers and I have a very limited acquaintance."

"I meant with the grounds." He pulled up some pictures on his phone and showed them to her.

She flipped through them. "Oh dear."

"Looks bad, doesn't it? It's gone wild. All that's been done is mowing the grass. The shrubs need to be brought under control, the weeds banished, and curb appeal added. I would like to subcontract that part of the job to you."

Kaylee thought of the Ashfords' big rambling house, dark green with crisp white window frames and flower boxes. The porch used to have white rocking chairs that were the perfect place to eat root beer snow cones. The backyard had the best swing set Kaylee had ever played on, with a slide that curved and had a roof over part of it. At least that's how she always thought of it as a child. For a few deliciously scary seconds, you were in the dark.

"I'd love to work on his house." Kaylee could feel her hands yearning to get dirty as she pulled weeds, trimmed shrubs, and planted flowers. She was already visualizing a plan for the place. "I'll draw a schematic for you."

"Don't worry about that. I trust you. Whatever you do will be great, especially when compared to what's there now or what I would have done."

Reese sat facing the door of the coffee shop. When it opened and Reese's eyes went wide and wary, Kaylee turned and saw Lorelei Lewis, romance writer, walking in with all the va-va-voom of an actress entering stage left. Of course the scent of the woman's perfume fighting with the aroma of Jessica's chocolate masterpieces was the biggest clue of all.

"Protect me! Please!" Reese whispered to Kaylee even as he rose to greet Lorelei who rushed toward him, arms outstretched.

"My darling Reese!" Lorelei enveloped the man in a dramatic hug. The look on his face as he looked at Kaylee over Lorelei's shoulder made her laugh out loud.

"Some help you are," he mouthed, making her laugh harder.

Lorelei drew back, running her hands down Reese's arms and grabbing his hands. "I've missed you so, Reese! I had to return to see if you've come to your senses yet and are willing to declare your undying love for me."

Reese pulled a hand free and patted her gingerly on the shoulder. "Nice to see you again, Mrs. Loblinski."

Lorelei stepped back with a shout of laughter, and Lorie Loblinski—a slightly chubby lady in slightly tight jeans and a long-sleeved knit shirt—appeared. "Well done! Nothing deflates Lorelei quicker than being called Mrs. Loblinski."

"Still drinking the usual?" Jessica called from behind the counter.

"Sure am," Lorie called back. "And I'll have one of those muffins Kaylee's eating." She turned to Kaylee. "Is it as good as it looks?"

"Better. Nice to see you again, Lorie, but aren't you ashamed, scaring Reese to death like that?"

She flicked a hand, waving away Kaylee's concern. "He's a big boy. He can take it."

"I don't know. He looks a bit pale to me."

Lorie took a seat next to Reese. "I hear you've got the job of readying Porter Ashford's house for sale."

Reese blinked. "I got the call less than two hours ago. How did—"

Lorie preened. "I have my ways."

"Small town, Reese, remember?" Jessica brought over the coffee and muffin.

Lorie took a sip and hummed with pleasure. "No one does it like you, Jessica. How's your handsome husband?"

"He's fine."

"Just fine?" Lorelei quirked an eyebrow.

Jessica returned the look. "Wonderful. Terrific. Excellent. What do you want me to say, Lorie? Luke's a great guy—as you well know."

"That's more like it, sweetie. Love the enthusiasm. We've got to appreciate our men while we have them." As Lorelei, she gave a dramatic sigh and put her hand to her heart. "It's a constant pain that my Dennis moved on all those years ago." Lorie reappeared with a sigh that seemed genuine and sad. "The louse."

Kaylee managed to swallow the last of her muffin without choking. The faculty dining room had never been this interesting.

The café door opened again and in walked three men and two women.

"Hey, Shannon, you finally made it," Lorie called.

"Got in on the 1:45 ferry."

"That's Shannon O'Mara," Lorie told her table mates. "A new Coterie member on my recommendation. The girl is a wonderful writer. Women's fiction. Family conflict. Bad blood between friends. Tragic illnesses. Buckets of tears. With our connections and her talent, she should make lots of lovely money."

"How nice for her."

Lorie grinned at Kaylee's sardonic tone. "Not that it's really up to us. We can introduce her to a couple of agents and editors, but it's readers who have to embrace her. I think they will."

Kaylee studied Shannon O'Mara, an ordinary-looking young woman whose unprepossessing appearance apparently hid a great talent. "Is that what the Coterie does? Help new writers?"

"We do that once in a while. Porter helped me. He introduced me to his agent who in turn introduced me to one of the top romance agents in New York. Mostly at Coterie meetings we write and encourage each other and sit around plotting murder and mayhem for our characters. For two weeks a year we're with others who understand that often our fictional worlds are more alive to us than our real worlds. None of us cares if one of us stays up all night writing and sleeps all day. To us that's normal. So is muttering to yourself, having conversations with invisible people, downing impossible amounts of coffee, and forgetting to eat."

"Did Mr. Ashford introduce Ward Meacham around too?"

Lorie's smile turned sad. "I still miss Porter. Wonderful man. He loved his Harriet. Terrific woman." She stood and spoke as Lorelei. "I must go join my fellow creatives for a lovely and lively conversation. *Au revoir, mes amis.*"

With a pat on Kaylee's hand and a kiss on Reese's cheek, Lorie left them. Reese watched her as she joined the Coterie group. "That wasn't too bad. I think you kept her under control."

"That part about you declaring your undying love for her wasn't too bad?"

He shrugged. "I do find it unnerving. I've got aunts her age."

Kaylee watched with bemusement as a flamboyant Lorelei embraced each of her fellow Coterie members, but it was Lorie who dropped into a chair and began talking with them.

"You asked about Ward Meacham. He's part of that group?" Reese practically rubbed his hands together at the thought. "He's coming to Orcas?"

"He was a member of the Coterie before he became famous, and yes, he's coming to Orcas. He'll be at the signing on Saturday."

"I love his stuff, especially his first book. It'll be fun to meet him."

They rose and went to the register to pay, then walked out together. They were halfway down the front steps when Kaylee realized Lorie hadn't answered her question about Porter helping Ward. Instead she had praised Porter and his wife. Had it been purposeful sidestepping, or merely a comment on what she considered more worthy?

Reese paused by his black pickup. "Are you free now or this evening to look over the Ashford property with me? After seven years of nothing, they want it fixed up yesterday so they can put it on the market immediately."

"How about this evening? I'd like to finish up what I was working on at the shop when you stopped in. When I go home for dinner, maybe Grandma will have some pictures of Mr. Ashford's place, and I can bring them to show you how fine it used to be."

"That'd be wonderful. Maybe around seven thirty? With the long summer evenings, we should have plenty of time to look around."

"Porter and Harry—Harriet—were our best friends." Bea sat across the table from Kaylee on the blue-and-white patio she'd always loved. White table, white chairs, blue cushions and rug. A huge, salmon *Pelargonium peltatum* in a giant, blue ceramic pot sat by a pair of blue rockers. Her grandmother had tended that ivy-leaf geranium for years, bringing it inside to lie dormant all winter, then taking it out into the sun each spring. In appreciation of her care, it grew and flowered profusely.

The best part of sitting out here was the view beyond the fence that edged the yard. The meadow was awash with lavender, colorful wildflowers, and waving grasses. *Soothing* was the best word Kaylee could think of to describe the vista. When the breeze blew the scent of the lavender, she could close her eyes and feel as if she were floating.

Tonight, however, was a time of purpose, not peace and rest.

"We used to go camping together when our families were young. Look." Bea held out the picture she'd just pulled from a box of old photos they'd lugged onto the back deck. "Your mom and Ursula after they went sliding in the mud."

Two little girls smiled happily for the camera, their teeth the only part of them not liberally smeared with brown slime. In the background stood Jules, maybe six or seven, arms crossed as he glared at the girls.

Kaylee studied the unhappy boy. "Was he always like that?"

"Always. Ed and I could never figure it out. Porter and Harry were wonderful people, warm, humorous, and good-natured. So were Isaac and Ursula. Jules was the oddball. He was always critical, squashing everyone's joy, and after Harry died when he was around twenty, he took pessimism to a whole new level. And then he brought Bettina home." Bea shuddered. "Poor Porter."

Kaylee grabbed the handful of pictures she'd culled from the lot and stood. "I've got to go or I'll be late to meet Reese."

"Have fun," she said absently, lost in her memories.

"I shouldn't be late. Bear, you're going to keep Grandma company."

Bear aimed his version of the evil eye at her. She laughed and gave him a good-bye scratch and a treat, which eased his doggy scowl considerably. "Bye, Grandma."

"Mm-hm." She was staring at a picture of herself with her husband standing in their motor launch. He had an arm slung around her shoulders, and huge smiles lit both their faces as he held up an enormous fish. With a deep sigh, Bea reached out and stroked his face.

Blinking back tears, Kaylee walked to her car. Had someone purposely taken her grandfather's life, ripping him from the woman who adored him? Accidents were heart-stopping, but they were accidents. Unintentional. Murder was doubly cruel in its deliberateness.

Reese was already at the Ashford house when she arrived, his pickup parked in front of the detached garage. He was in the front yard studying the place. It needed painting, its once vibrant deep green now faded. The white, wooden window frames were peeling, some of the screens were ripped, and one of the front shutters had come loose and dangled, like someone hanging on to a cliff's edge by one hand.

The foundation shrubs—mostly *Rhododendron strigillosum* and *Rhododendron tsutsusi* with some low-growing *Cedrus deodara*—had gone wild. The rhododendron had grown so high it covered several of the windows, and the azaleas needed their hair cut and shaped. The cedar grew out into the yard and had been clipped off by the lawn mower. The only thing that looked the way it should was the *Cercis canadensis*, though the eastern redbud looked a bit out of place, so well-behaved among the other wild shrubs.

"This garden must have been amazing a couple of months ago when the rhodys and azaleas and that eastern redbud were all blooming," Kaylee observed. A few blown and browned blooms still sagged from some of the shrubs. "Pinks, purples, rose, and that unique color of the redbud. Beautiful."

"It really was. I think long-blooming flowers are nicer though," Reese said. "Of course I need to give you a better backdrop. Those windows need scraping and painting, and I'll need to tack the shutters in place."

Kaylee studied the rampant growth. "Are you sure you want me to tackle the landscaping? I don't have much experience in that area."

"Absolutely. You'll do a great job, I'm sure of it. With you making the grounds gorgeous, and me making the house sound— I'm concerned about the roof—this place should sell in no time."

She frowned at him. "You're sure you want me for this job?"

"Sure. Your grandmother says you have an artist's eye, and I know you know about plants."

"I can identify all kinds of plants and flowers and classify them. I'm an arranger of plant facts more than the arranger of actual plants in an aesthetic and attractive way."

"You're not creating a new landscaping design. You're taking what's here and making it neat and attractive. Trim and prune, add some annuals for color. All the Ashfords want is for the place to look attractive to buyers." He smiled absently. "I know you can do it. Should the front door be black or white?"

"White." She still felt uncertain. This job would be one more new thing on top of many others. "I got fired from my job at the university." Which had nothing to do with the current conversation. She flushed.

"Yeah, I heard." But he didn't seem bothered by it. "Bea said it was more about the university's issues than you not being good at what you did. I'd like to work with you. What do you say?"

"I say—" She gasped. "Oh no! Look!"

# 7

"What?" Reese spun around and scanned where she pointed. "What am I looking at?"

"See that plant there among the azaleas?"

"The one with the feathery leaves and white flowers? Carrot, right?"

She stared at him. "You know wild carrot?"

"My mom planted a large vegetable garden, and one of my jobs was harvesting stuff for dinner. The carrots had those feathery leaves."

Kaylee was impressed. "A lot of people don't even know carrots have leaves, let alone what they look like."

"Isn't it also called Queen Anne's lace?"

"You know that?" The man was amazing.

"My mom again. She'd pick it and put the stems in colored water, and the color would go up the stems into the flowers. My brother and I both did that with carnations for our science projects in elementary school. We both got As."

Kaylee laughed. "But you don't know quite enough in this case."

"How so?"

"That may look like wild carrot, but it's *Conium maculatum*."

"Surely you jest." He looked at her in mock horror, then grinned. "I don't know what that means."

"Poison hemlock."

His eyes went wide. "What? The stuff that killed Socrates?"

"The very same." She walked to the plant tucked cozily in the harmless house plantings. She grabbed his arm when he reached out to pull it up. "Don't touch it. All parts of it are poisonous. You need to wear gloves and protective clothes to deal with it."

"Poisonous enough to kill you?"

"If you ingest enough."

"And how are the Ashfords lucky enough to have a poisonous plant growing in their garden? Maybe Jules was having an extra grumpy day and sowed it."

"It grows wild on Orcas. It grows wild in lots of places, including meadows where livestock eat it and die. Sometimes people eat it because they think they've found wild carrot. The tuber on the poison hemlock looks like the tuber of a wild carrot or parsnip. Some have cut up the leaves and added them to salad greens."

"Sounds sort of like picking the wrong mushroom."

"Exactly."

"How can you tell the difference?"

"The hemlock has purple spots on a smooth stem and the flowers aren't as compact as the Queen Anne's lace, which usually has a small red flower in the middle of all the white." She grinned at him. "It's supposed to look like a drop of Queen Anne's blood. It also has hairy stems. Keep that in mind so you don't mishandle some when I'm not around to save you." She grinned, then surveyed the green chaos before her. "I hope I can make the place look good for Isaac and Ursula. They deserve it after all they've been through."

His smile was warm, and she felt it all the way to her toes. "I'm not the least bit worried." He stepped back from the garden and studied the house again. "It's amazing what seven years of neglect can do to a place. I'm almost afraid to look inside. Do we dare?"

He pulled a key from his pocket and unlocked the front door. Kaylee followed him, even though her responsibilities were outside. She couldn't resist the lure of the place. In spite of the musty smell of a house shut for too long, it was like coming home.

"It looks just as I remember it." She ran a hand over the back of the couch. "I don't know what I expected—maybe the chaos of the outside brought inside—but it looks so familiar and unchanged."

"You're seeing the furniture and the obvious." Reese poked at a windowsill on which sat a dead African violet. He lifted the violet to study the sill. "The unseen—that's where the damage will be."

Kaylee took the plant from him. "*Saintpaulia ionantha*. Poor thing is gone beyond saving." She looked around for a wastebasket. Finding none in the living room, she trailed Reese as he walked into the kitchen.

Mugs stood upside down in a dish drainer, spoons spiking up from the drainer's silverware compartment. A ceramic pot full of cooking utensils sat by the stove, and salt and pepper shakers shaped like the dragons in Porter's *They Came Alone* guarded the table by the bow window. Kaylee remembered the night he'd brought Bea a set of the dragons when he came to dinner.

"Giveaways for the big book fair," he'd said. "Other people give mugs and pens. I get to give salt and pepper shakers that look like Ondor and Violine. How cool is that?" And all the adults had laughed. Twelve-year-old Kaylee had begged her grandmother for the dragons and had them sitting on her desk for years. They were still tucked away somewhere in her unpacked boxes.

"How did Porter die?" Reese looked under the sink and nodded in satisfaction. Kaylee took that to mean no leaks.

"Grandma said he fell down the stairs from the second floor to the front hall. He lay there a couple of days before he was found. I think a guy named Howie found him. If I remember right, he was a teacher who came to Orcas every summer to write the next Great American Novel. He came to talk writing and found Mr. Ashford's body." Kaylee frowned as she turned a slow circle. *Where are the wastebaskets in this house?* "You can ask Grandma if you want to know more about what happened. She'll know the details."

"Maybe I will." Reese opened the refrigerator and Kaylee saw desiccated globs of what had once been food sitting on the shelves. "At least we don't have to worry about that mess. Isaac will have a housecleaning team come in after we're finished." He walked from the room.

"Grandma wanted to come in after the funeral and take care of things like the refrigerator and leftover food stuffs in the cupboards and any laundry left in the hamper. You know, the daily life stuff that needs cleaning up. In typical fashion Jules had the house locked and refused to let anyone in for any reason. Grandma and Grandpa were hurt and miffed at being denied that final service for their dear friend. It was like Jules thought they'd take things. As if they would."

Reese brushed a cobweb off his shoulder and face, which had been collected when he'd leaned into the hall closet. "Makes me glad my contact person is Isaac."

They wandered into what had been Porter's office. His large wooden desk sat under the front windows. A mug of pens and pencils sat to the left of a brass lamp, and a compartmentalized tray full of paper clips, rubber bands, sticky notes, and other office supplies sat to the right. Kaylee thought of her desk at the university with its ever-growing pile of to-be-read journals, papers, and lab reports. And that was a small drop compared to the ocean of material on her computer. Her shoulders tightened just thinking of the pressure to read and absorb it all.

*But no more*, she reminded herself. She was free from that

burden. She forced herself to relax, to take a deep breath. That impossible weight was no longer on her shoulders.

She set the dead violet beside the laptop, leaned against the desk, and shook her head in disbelief. "This isn't right."

Reese looked up from examining what appeared to be a water stain on the hardwood floor. "What isn't?" He studied the ceiling, where a discoloration made him frown.

"How did the office get so neat? It's not like I remember. I remember clutter and papers and mail and stuff. You know, basic office chaos. I mean, if Jules wouldn't let anyone in . . ."

"Maybe he got tidier in his later years."

Kaylee wandered about the room. Two walls had bookshelves filled with volumes of all sorts. She saw research books, how-to-write books, history books, fantasy novels by Porter's competitors in the cutthroat world of publishing, and one section filled with his own titles, both hardback and paperback, arranged by publication date. Foreign language editions occupied their own space right beside audio versions both abridged and unabridged.

The fourth wall of the room was floor-to-ceiling windows looking out on the pond and meadow beyond the house. A much-used overstuffed chair faced the meadow. A lamp sat alone on the end table to its left. Kaylee shut her eyes and in memory saw half-empty mugs of cold coffee with creamer skins on top, printouts with notes scribbled on them sitting in an untidy stack, a freezer bag half full of cookies for "whenever," and numerous pens and mechanical pencils on the end table. A stack of novels to be read, their haphazard arrangement defying gravity, sat beside the chair. She opened her eyes and saw only the lamp.

She wandered over and stared out the window. "They used to have sheep in that meadow. White with black faces. Grandpa brought me up once to see a new lamb when we came to the island for Easter. They let me hold it." She smiled. "Cutest little thing."

"Things like that stay with you, don't they?" He was studying the stain on the ceiling again. "I'm going to need the plumber if this water damage is from a leaky pipe instead of a bad roof."

"I remember ducks trailed by their ducklings floating across that pond." Kaylee sighed at the memories and turned to look for a wastebasket for the *Saintpaulia ionantha*. She couldn't leave it on the pristine desk and ruin the room's perfection. But even a tidy office should have a basket. Maybe especially a tidy office. Of course so should a kitchen, and it had none.

As she looked on the far side of the desk, she bumped the ergonomic desk chair tucked neatly in the knee well. It rolled away from the desk on its plastic carpet protector. She grabbed it and turned to push it back in place when she saw her prize, lost in the shadows of the deep kneehole. She reached under and pulled out a black plastic container whose size would take a large kitchen trash bag if it had a trash bag, which it didn't. As she prepared to drop the violet in, she noticed some crumpled papers in the bottom.

She frowned, The bit of clutter struck her as an anomaly in this super-neat room. She turned in a circle. "Did Isaac mention whether anyone has been here to get Mr. Ashford's personal papers and such?" Maybe someone they trusted more than Kaylee's grandparents had been allowed in.

"Isaac said none of the family has been to the house since before his father died. They didn't even come inside after the funeral."

"Probably because Jules made such an issue of things. Grandma hosted the funeral meal at her place, and she said Jules was being so disagreeable about what he thought was the unfairness of the will that everyone left on the first ferry they could. And they haven't been back."

Reese turned from the water stain to the bookshelf and

scanned book titles. "It's amazing how one fly in the ointment like Jules . . ."

"Or Bettina."

"Or Bettina—can make all the efforts of the peacemakers come to nothing." He pulled a book off the shelf and held it out to Kaylee. "Ever read this one?"

"*The Mere Mention?* The evil magician Scavarrd gave me nightmares for weeks." She shuddered.

"But Princess Patrizia . . ." He gave an exaggerated sigh.

"Please. She was colorless next to the amazing Mattius. Talk about a Renaissance man."

Reese blew dust off the spine and stuffed *The Mere Mention* back in place. "I wonder which kid got which books assigned in the will."

"We'll never know."

"Right. It's none of our business. Still I'd love to know what Isaac and Ursula finally gave in on to make Jules happy enough to end the standoff."

"I bet one of them took the book that's only a title and gave him one that has regular income." Kaylee turned another circle. "Doesn't it seem strange that there are no papers anywhere in this room? I mean, look around. Nothing. Have you ever seen an office this sterile? Shouldn't there be the general untidiness of a room much used and which no one has been in since Mr. Ashford died? It's not like he cleaned up everything and then went and fell down the stairs. I mean, even if he was neater after I knew him, there would still be *something.*"

"Um." Reese was studying the ceiling again. "I'm sorry, Kaylee. I've got to go upstairs and see where this water stain is coming from. The sooner these things are caught and fixed, the better."

She was barely aware of him leaving the room as she slowly

reached into the wastebasket and pulled out the crumpled, slightly yellowed sheets of paper. Slowly and carefully she straightened them, spreading them flat on the desk. Maybe they were something Isaac or Ursula would want. She knew she'd never offer them to Jules.

They looked like sheets of a manuscript printed out and then edited, like the papers that used to collect around the overstuffed chair by the window. On the first page she examined, pencil scribbles ran up one margin, and cross outs and additions marked the body of the text. Every page was similarly marked, the only difference being the amount of corrections made. The pages were numbered from 421 to 435.

A new book he had been working on? She read several pages and found its style very different from what she considered a typical Porter Ashford book—clever, imaginative, action-filled, and smooth with his great depth of insight into the human condition hidden in the plot so you only thought about it after you enjoyed the story.

These papers weren't part of a fantasy novel. No swords or sorcery, no dragons or dungeons, no perils or parallel universes. They read like a different kind of literary work, graceful and thoughtful, full of beautiful phrases and imaginative word choices instead of imaginative story lines.

Was he trying something different? Was this Jules's name-only book?

On a shelf near the desk sat a box of red manila folders. Convincing herself that taking one wasn't really stealing, Kaylee slid the crinkled sheets into a bright red folder.

Reese came thundering down the stairs. "Got to call a plumber. Nasty mess in the bathroom over that mark. I just hope there isn't a mold problem."

He wandered over to the shelf of Porter's hardbacks. He

pulled *They Came Alone* out, Ondor and Violine flying majestically across the cover, Scarlotte and King Reegon on their scaly backs. "I wanted a pet dragon when I finished this. I was about fourteen when I read it." He turned to put it back in place, then stopped. "What do we have here?"

# 8

Kaylee rushed to his side. "What?" She pictured a dead mouse or a giant spider, which she hoped Reese would dispatch quickly. Or maybe a money clip with lots of crisp bills. Or tattered bills. She'd take either. Not that she could actually take either, should money actually be there for some inexplicable reason. It would belong to the estate. But who hadn't dreamed of finding treasure?

Reese pulled out a thumb drive from behind *They Came Alone.* "This was just sitting there on the shelf behind the books."

Kaylee stared at the small black memory stick resting in Reese's hand. "I wonder what's on it."

"I don't know, but its contents are really none of our business." He heard himself and grimaced. "Sorry. I didn't mean to sound quite so stuffy." She was ready to wave aside his attitude when he smiled and added, "But it isn't ours."

She sighed as curiosity warred with ethics. "Killjoy. After all, we found it."

"If we're going to be accurate, *I* found it."

She wrinkled her nose at him. "Okay, *you* found it." An idea struck hard and fast. "But I bet I know what's on it."

"Assuming there's anything on it."

"I think it's the name-only book."

He frowned. "Jules's name-only book? The one he's been having a fit over because everyone thought it was just a title? That's a pretty big assumption, don't you think?"

"Probably, but it makes sense."

If anything Reese looked even more skeptical. "You're a conspiracy theorist."

"I'm not." She ignored his snort and held out the folder. "I found pages in the wastebasket. They're very different from Mr. Ashford's usual style, but they're wonderful. Absolutely wonderful. I bet there are more of them on that drive."

He flicked a finger at the folder. "Maybe they're not his papers at all. How's that for an idea?"

"Of course they're his. I found them in his house. In his wastebasket."

"Do they have his name on them?"

She opened the folder and checked to be certain she remembered correctly. There were only page numbers in the header. "No, but they have his handwritten corrections and rewrites."

"How do you know the writing's his?"

"I've seen it before when I came here with Grandpa. Mr. Ashford used to print out his work and do his editing in the margins and in between lines of the hard copy with a thin point marker. Then he'd correct the manuscript on the computer."

"Okay, maybe it is his handwriting, but that doesn't mean the original typed pages were his. They could be anyone's. Didn't he have other writers come here?"

"He did." Much as she hated admitting it, Reese had a point. "He was always helping others like he helped Lorelei. She says he got her started by introducing her to the right people. That guy Howie who found him probably wanted the same kind of help. I imagine there are lots of others."

Kaylee didn't like the idea of the papers belonging to someone else. She wanted that beautiful, evocative writing to be Porter's. "I guess the only thing to do is see what's on the drive. For all we know, it's blank."

He looked at her. "You're saying we should read someone's private work? That feels a lot like reading someone's mail. It's an invasion of privacy."

She studied the drive in his hand as she scrambled for an answer. "We wouldn't want to bother the family if it's nothing."

"Right." He rolled his eyes. "That's us, noble protectors of legatees."

She grinned at him. He seemed to be a great guy, even when he was playing devil's advocate and driving her nuts. Their eyes caught and held. She felt unexpected heat rush to her face and knew she resembled a clown with bright red spots on her cheeks. She forced herself to look away.

Self-consciously she cleared her suddenly dry throat and looked anywhere but at him. Her gaze fell on *They Came Alone*, back in its place on the shelf. She frowned. "Did the stick fall behind the books accidentally or was it hidden there on purpose?"

Reese looked from her to the bookshelf. "Why would you think it was hidden?" He gave a quick laugh. "I was right. You *are* a conspiracy theorist."

"I'm not. I think most things are exactly as they appear. But . . ." Kaylee looked around the pristine room. It always came back to the same thing. "It's just too neat. It's not right."

"I agree it doesn't look anything like my office, but that doesn't mean something's wrong."

Again the picture of the homey chaos she remembered flashed through her mind. "You didn't see this place when Mr. Ashford was alive. This is unnatural, and it would bother you too." She reached for the drive still sitting on his palm. "I'll put this in the folder with the papers."

Reese handed it to her. "Put it all in the desk drawer. I'll tell Isaac it's all there the next time I speak to him."

She opened the shallow center drawer of the desk and slid the folder inside.

Reese's attention shifted back to the water spot on the ceiling.

"I need to check upstairs again." He left the room, and she heard him clomp up the steps.

Her eyes narrowed as she stared at the desk. How could they just leave the papers and drive in that drawer? That *unlocked* drawer?

She pulled the drawer open and stared at the folder lying there so innocently. She shut the drawer and took a step back. Like Reese said, it wasn't her business. Both the papers and the drive had been safe here for years. They'd be safe a bit longer.

But they'd been hidden. Now they were lying where any nosy person could find them. She brushed aside the thought that the house was locked even if the drawer wasn't. There were bound to be break-ins, even in a sweet town like Turtle Cove. And abandoned houses like this one were easier targets.

She opened the drawer again and lifted the folder out. She could feel the bump the drive made. She'd just take them home with her to keep them safe. If anyone came looking, they'd never expect them to be at Wildflower Cottage.

She glanced at the ceiling. Reese didn't need to know.

She slid the empty drawer closed and tucked the folder under her shirt in case he came back before she escaped. She looked down at the strange rectangular shape outlined across her front. Like he wouldn't notice. Time to get out of here fast. She headed for the door.

"See you later, Reese!"

"Heading out already?"

"Yeah, I promised Grandma I wouldn't be long," she replied, hoping her voice didn't sound as guilty as she felt.

"All right. Have a good one!"

"You too!" And she fled, the mysterious folder feeling like fire against her skin.

As Kaylee drove home from the Ashfords', she was distracted from her thoughts about the jump drive and her questionable right to open it by a woman walking along the side of the narrow, winding road. She appeared as if by magic when Kaylee rounded a curve, wearing jeans, a dark shirt, and a sweater. It wasn't dusk yet, but in the gathering shadows, the woman was hard to see even with the headlights on. Kaylee hit the brakes. She reminded herself that if it wasn't women who were a danger along the road, it could be deer. The island was alive with them.

The woman appeared agitated, her arms flailing as if she was having an animated conversation with herself. As Kaylee pulled even with her, the woman glanced over. It was Lorelei Lewis. Or Lorie Loblinski. Kaylee slowed to a crawl and lowered the window.

"Lorie, are you all right?"

Lorie jerked as if she'd been unaware of the red SUV pulling up beside her. She peered at the car. "Who is it?"

"It's me, Kaylee Bleu."

Lorie straightened her shoulders as if trying to channel Lorelei, but she couldn't quite manage it. She slumped again.

"Can I give you a lift?" Kaylee didn't like the idea of Lorie being out alone in the gathering night. Another driver might not see her, dressed as she was in dark clothes. "I'd be happy to take you wherever you're going."

Lorie looked around and frowned. "I didn't realize how far I walked."

"You're staying at Turtle Cove Inn, right?" Kaylee jerked a thumb over her shoulder. "It's back that way."

"You're right. I need to go back to the inn."

Kaylee pushed open the passenger door. "Climb in. You can't walk along the side of the road in all that black. You're too hard to see."

Lorie looked at her sweater-clad arm. "Huh? Never thought of that." She climbed in the car and slumped in the seat.

Kaylee pulled into the first drive she came to and turned around. She felt the woman's distress envelop the car like a fog rolling off the sea. "What's wrong? Want to talk about it?"

Lorie never lifted her eyes. "No. It won't help."

They drove in silence for about ten seconds. Then Lorie sighed and turned to Kaylee. "I'm so mad and so upset I don't know what to do. And it's all my own fault." The last was a muted wail. Lorie paused, then corrected herself. "Well, maybe not *all*, but mostly."

"I'm sorry." What else was there to say?

Lorie sighed again. "I guess it's too late to start disciplining a twenty-year-old, don't you think?"

"I do and it probably is." It would be fascinating to meet the twenty-year-old who had Lorie so upset.

"I should have started a long time ago. Like twenty years ago."

Kaylee made a noncommittal humming sound.

"But she was so adorable when she stamped her foot and said, 'No!' That's *no* with an exclamation point. Always an exclamation point. So cute! Little red curls dancing and those beautiful green eyes sparking. Sort of Shirley Temple without the dimple and the smile. It was all I could do not to laugh at how adorable she was. How could I possibly discipline her? Then she was five and I admired her independent spirit when she stood up to me." Lorie's unhappy smile had a wry twist. "See? My fault."

"Strong-willed kids can be a handful." Not that Kaylee knew from parental experience, but she'd seen them all too often in classes.

Lorie snorted. "Understatement. They take aim at whatever they desire with the single-mindedness of a bullet heading for a target. Nothing will stop them when they put their minds to something." She paused, raised the index fingers of both hands. "Strong-willed. Bullet. Target. I've got to remember that metaphor. It's a good one."

Trees flashed by, their foliage making the dusk deeper, the encroaching night darker. As they drove past a meadow, Kaylee saw a small herd of deer feeding. *Stay there, guys.* They were so picturesque and lovely when they weren't decorating the front grill of a car.

Lorie sighed. "When I started making money from my writing, I hired household help. The girl never had to make her bed or pick up after herself. All she had to do was ask for something, and it was done. It was hers. And then she was thirteen. You ever lived with a thirteen-year-old girl?"

Kaylee shook her head.

"Lucky you. Then there's fifteen. Sixteen. She became an expert at getting whatever she wanted, saying whatever she felt no matter how much it hurt, a master at ignoring anything she didn't like—like her mother. Now she's twenty, and she gives willful a whole new meaning."

Kaylee thought of some of the twenty-year-olds she'd taught at the university. They were surprised when she gave them zeros for work not turned in. "But I planned to do it," they said as if she should grade them on their unrealized intentions. Or they were shocked when they got a poor grade for sloppy or incomplete papers. "But I tried," they'd said as if she should give them a gold star and write *good job* beside the star because they tried. Apparently no one told them that *trying* was not a synonym for *doing.* Instead they'd been coddled and told any effort, no matter how sloppy, was wonderful. Maybe at five it was wonderful, but as a college student it was deplorable. Ruinous.

Lorie rubbed the back of her neck. "Her trouble—and mine—is she's still stamping her foot, and it isn't cute anymore."

No, entitled twenty-year-olds were not cute, no matter how attractive they were.

Lorie laid her head against the rest and closed her eyes. They popped open and she turned to Kaylee. "You do flowers."

Kaylee nodded, surprised at the abrupt change of topic.

"You can help us. I told her it was too last-minute, but of course she won't listen. Strong-willed. Bullet. Target. You could help us. After all, you and Bea are my friends. Friends always help friends, right?"

Kaylee squinted into the gathering gloom. She and Lorie were friends? Interesting.

"It's on Saturday," Lorie said. "Saturday evening. Somewhere."

"What's on Saturday?"

"The wedding."

Wedding? "You're getting married Saturday?"

Lorie looked at Kaylee, a horrified expression on her face. "*I'm* not getting married. Where'd you ever get that preposterous idea?"

Since she had no answer, Kaylee kept quiet.

"It's Melanie. She showed up on the ferry this afternoon with Ryan the Loser in tow and wants a perfect wedding on Saturday. On Saturday! She even brought a dress!"

"A wedding dress?"

"A princess-y one with flowing skirts and sparkles all over. No surprise there." Lorie smiled briefly. "I have to admit it's beautiful. The wretched girl has always had great taste. Expensive, but great. She won't tell me how much the dress cost."

"I take it the wedding is a surprise to you."

"It most definitely is." The righteous indignation was back full bore. "And she wants to marry Ryan the Loser!"

"Really? That bad?"

Lorie growled. There was no other word for the sound that came out of her throat.

"What does he do for a living?"

Lorie's burst of laughter dripped with sarcasm. "Do? Ryan? How should I know? He doesn't talk. When Melanie introduced us last month, I gave him a week at most. She's vibrant and fun, and he's . . ." She searched for a word and couldn't find one. "I think he wants my money."

Kaylee blinked. "You make that much that someone would marry your daughter to get their hands on it some day in the far, far future?" It slipped out before she could bite it back. "Sorry. Not my business."

"You're right. It isn't. But I don't mind telling you I do very well, especially since I've put up my backlist as e-books. I'm a hybrid." She said it as if it were something to be proud of.

"What's a hybrid?" Kaylee was pretty sure Lorie wasn't speaking of cars.

"I have a traditional publisher, and I also do independent projects. I enjoy the fruits of both worlds. But surely you know this. You've published too."

Kaylee had. "I think there's a big difference between academic publish-or-perish projects and commercial fiction."

Lorie clearly wasn't interested in discussing those differences. "You know what really makes me furious? This is supposed to be *my* time, these two weeks on Orcas. This time with the Coterie is the highlight of my year. We brainstorm. We talk craft. We talk marketing. We brag about our agents. We grind our publishers beneath our collective heel. She knows that! And she has the gall to show up in the middle of my time! Can you believe it?"

From the other things Lorie had said about her daughter, Kaylee could. "So you only have three days to plan this perfect wedding." Even never-married Kaylee knew weddings were logistical nightmares that took months to plan.

Lorie smiled brightly and patted Kaylee's hand. "And you're Part One of the plan. Flowers. Thanks for agreeing to do them."

Kaylee had no memory of agreeing to any such thing. "Let me talk to my grandmother."

She meant it as a check for the viability of such a commitment on extremely short notice, but Lorie heard it as a consult for the best ideas.

"Wonderful," she said. "I know you and Bea will create a floral feast for the eyes and make Melanie—and by extension me—happy."

Kaylee turned into the drive at the Turtle Cove Inn. Instead of climbing out of the car as Kaylee expected, Lorie settled in. "Who do you recommend for the food? And where should we go for a beautiful setting with a lovely vista? Who can be the officiant? And what about a good photographer?"

"I don't know, Lorie. I just moved here."

Lorie waved that small bit of information aside. "You know more people than you think. How about the Petal Pushers?"

"Maybe they can help." Did they do things like arrange last-minute weddings? "You'll have to speak to them. They're already committed to helping with the book signing at Between the Lines."

"That's in the morning. Melanie wants the wedding in the evening."

*And what Melanie wants* . . . "You'll have to talk to them," Kaylee repeated. "Why not have the reception here at the inn?"

Lorie studied the exterior of the facility. "Good idea. They like me. I'm a good annual customer, and so are the other members of the Coterie. The inn's owners love us. But where should we have the ceremony itself?"

"There are several churches on the island. Maybe one of them is available."

"Melanie wants outside with a sweeping vista."

"Again I can't help you. I don't know vistas yet. All I know is Wildflower Cottage."

Lorie jumped on what she saw as a possibility. "Where's Wildflower Cottage? Does it have a vista? If it's anything like its name, it sounds just the thing. We can check it out in the morning."

"It's my grandmother's home. My home."

"You'd let us have the wedding at your house? Kaylee, how wonderful! Thank you."

Kaylee once again didn't remember agreeing, but she no longer wondered where Melanie had gotten her strong will. Bullet. Target. "I'd have to charge." There might as well be some benefit to this manipulation. "After all, it's a major inconvenience, and my grandmother isn't a young woman."

"Right. An old lady. I get it. The fee is no problem. *If* Melanie likes it."

Maybe Melanie wouldn't like it. Kaylee could only hope. Then she thought of the meadow washed in the golden light of the magic hour and knew there wasn't a chance in the world Melanie would say no.

Bubbling with plans, Lorie finally climbed from the car. "You are a wonderful woman, Kaylee Bleu. A wonderful woman."

Kaylee drove home in the dark, not at all convinced Bea would agree with Lorie's assessment when she learned her backyard was to be a wedding location.

"Why not?" Bea said.

"But—"

"But nothing. It's beautiful back there. Let the girl enjoy it. There's that lovely arbor in the storeroom at The Flower Patch. You can drape it with tulle and string it with fairy lights. You can rent chairs and covers. I bet Melanie wants covers on the chairs. It sounds like whatever's most expensive is what that girl will want."

Kaylee felt the taut muscles in her neck relax. "I'm so glad you're here to help me."

Her grandmother held up a finger. "I didn't say that. My days as a wedding planner are over. I don't have time to help. I'm packing for a big move."

Kaylee felt panic clamp around her chest so tightly she couldn't draw a deep breath. "But I've never done a wedding before." She'd never organized any large event before. She organized plants into neat classifications, following established protocols, and the plants stayed where she put them. They never demanded anything of her or expected her to do unfamiliar things. "I don't even know where to begin. It's not like I had a wedding of my own to learn from."

"Three little words—no, four: Mary, Jess, DeeDee, and Reese."

"Lorie mentioned them too. You really think they'll help?"

"I think they'll love it. At least the women will."

"I can definitely ask Mary. She works for you."

"For you," Bea corrected.

"That still seems so weird. I mean, I've always worked for people, not people for me.

But the others? I can't impose."

"Sure you can. They are lovely people who will become your very good friends." Bea grinned. "And I'm going to teach you how it's done." She cleared her throat and became feeble before Kaylee's eyes, shoulders collapsing inward, head weaving on a neck suddenly too weak to hold it up.

"Oh, Kaylee!" Her voice quaked. "I'm so overwhelmed! This move is so hard. So stressful. I'm running out of time to get everything ready before the movers come, and I still have so much to do." She looked at Kaylee with exaggerated despair. "Would you help an old lady? Please?"

Kaylee laughed. "Like I can play the old lady card. And if I looked at them with an expression like that, they'd run far and fast."

Bea straightened and grinned. "They'll help you, sweetheart. The women are Petal Pushers, and sweet Reese has a built-in helpful gene." She looked at Kaylee and must have seen all the uncertainty. Her eyes softened. "I'll help too."

Kaylee blew out a huge sigh of relief. "You will? I feel like I can breathe again."

"Don't relax too much, my girl. I'll get the time back by putting you to work for me at the cottage."

# 9

Thursday morning Kaylee stood in the front hall and watched her grandmother pull coat after coat from the front closet. She gave each a quick look, then dropped it in the growing pile on the floor. Bear prowled around the garments, sniffing, sticking his head into the heap as if he expected to find a small, furry creature he could vanquish to great praise.

Kaylee studied the pile and pretended shock. "Grandma! I don't think I know anyone with this many coats. You've got way more than me."

Bea looked at the pile at her feet and shrugged. "I've got way more years than you. For a long time I had to buy new ones because I kept gaining weight. Then I got older and started losing weight, but the old ones were out of style. I had to get more new ones. This pile is a life history. Anthropologists should analyze it in a study of the typical American woman, sort of like historians examine potsherds to learn about ancient civilizations."

Kaylee laughed. "You are anything but typical, believe me."

"I should hope so. Open the trash bag so we can stuff these in to go to the Help Center."

"Aren't you going to keep a couple?"

"I'm going to Arizona. You don't need coats in Arizona."

"It depends on where in Arizona you're going. It has mountains and snow as well as desert and heat."

"Tucson has heat."

Kaylee pulled out her phone and pushed a few commands. "Heat is right. 100 degrees in June and July, but 65 in December and January. And that's the high. It's quite cool in the night."

Bea looked surprised. "Okay. I'll take this blue one, the gray one, and the black boiled wool. Stuff the rest in the white trash bags."

Kaylee began doing as told. She was folding a handsome navy peacoat when her grandmother's sigh drew her attention. "What's wrong?"

Bea held a worn, red barn jacket over her arm, its leather collar worn of color and its cuffs frayed. She ran her hand over it as if she were petting a much-loved pup. "I'm taking this with me."

Kaylee thought of the picture of her grandparents on their boat with her grandfather displaying his big fish. He'd been wearing the red jacket.

"This old coat was his favorite." Bea held it to her cheek. "He'd come in wearing it, looking like some homeless man on the corner, and I'd tell him I was going to throw it away. 'It's embarrassing me that you're seen in public in that thing,' I'd say. 'Sweet Bea,' he'd say back, 'you're the only thing I love more than this jacket. Do not—I repeat, do *not* try to sneak it out of the house.' And he'd kiss me and hang it in the closet. 'I'm getting the trash bag,' I'd say and start for the kitchen. He'd grab me and kiss me again." Her eyes filled with tears. "Not that I'd ever throw it away. It was just a silly game we played."

Kaylee felt herself blinking back tears too. The look of yearning in her grandmother's eyes for what had been and was no more made Kaylee ache for her. It also made her long for a love as deep and wide as the affection her grandparents had had for each other.

"It's funny." Bea continued to pet the coat. "Every time I think of Ed going out on the water, he's wearing this coat." She hugged it close, then took it and the other coats she had decided to keep into the bedroom where she was organizing her packing. Kaylee watched her go, her own heart heavy. If they only knew what had happened to him!

She folded the last coat, slid it into a white garbage bag, and grabbed a black marker. She wrote *coats* across the bag in large letters and put the bag with several others for a trip to the Help Center.

The doorbell rang, making Kaylee jump and Bear bark. *Who is here so early?*

"That's Reese," Bea called. "Will you let him in?"

Kaylee pulled the door open to a scruffy and very handsome Reese. Today his T-shirt was gray and his flannel shirt was a gray, blue, and red plaid, but the blue Dodgers cap was the same.

"Good morning." Kaylee told herself her big smile was natural when a friend came to visit, but she didn't fool herself. She was, after all, a PhD. "Want some coffee?"

He followed her to the kitchen where they were joined by an all-business Bea. Her vulnerable moment over the red barn coat might never have been. She poured herself a cup of coffee.

"Reese," she said, "I have a motorboat in storage at the marina. It's been in storage since Ed went away. I want you to check it out and make sure it's in good shape for Kaylee."

Kaylee stared at her grandmother. "You're giving me your boat?" She'd assumed it had been sold long ago.

"You can't live on an island without a boat." She reconsidered. "Well, you can. I'm a case in point. I might as well not have had one for all the use I gave it, which is none for the last five years. But it's better to own one."

"I know. I figured I'd buy one eventually. I never thought about you giving me yours."

"Why buy if mine's still okay?" Bea frowned. "Of course you may not like it."

"Is it the same one Grandpa had when I was a kid? I liked that one."

"No, this one was only a couple of years old when he went away. It's practically brand new since it's been protected all this time."

"And it was driven by a little old lady who only went to church and the grocery store, right?"

Bea frowned at her. "Katherine Leigh, are you saying I sound like some used car salesman?"

Kaylee put her arm around her grandmother's shoulder and kissed her cheek. "You sound like someone who loves me and is being nicer than I deserve."

"True, especially about the nicer part," Bea said, tweaking Kaylee's nose. "But you may want a bigger boat, being a young person and all."

Kaylee smiled. Her grandmother made her sound about sixteen. "I don't need big. That's a guy thing."

"Hey!" Reese looked over from giving a delighted Bear an ear scratch.

Kaylee grinned at him, then turned back to her grandmother. "It floats and it has a motor, right? What more do I need?"

"It does have a good-sized motor, though I forget its horsepower. Don't assume anything else about its condition. That's why Reese is here." Bea poured half-and-half into her mug and watched her coffee lighten. "I asked Yancy at the marina to get the boat out of dry storage. He assures me it's running well, but I want Reese to go over everything with you. I want to know if you like it enough to make it yours or if I should just sell it."

"Is it the boat in the picture of you and Grandpa and the big fish?"

"The big fish?" Bea looked at her with pity. "That's a salmon, Kaylee."

Kaylee shrugged. "I do plants, not fish."

"Reese, when I'm gone, you'll have to teach her about fish."

He stood by the big window, a happy Bear tucked under his arm like a football. "My pleasure."

Suddenly fish didn't look so uninteresting.

"Now off you two go." Bea made shooing motions with her hands. "And Bear. Take him too. Check out that launch."

"But The Flower Patch." Kaylee saw the day spinning away with her accomplishing none of her pressing tasks. "We've got that last-minute wedding, remember?"

Bea shot her a dirty look. "Of course I remember. I'm old, not senile. While you go to the marina, I'll go into the shop and start working on things with Mary."

Kaylee accepted the inevitable. "Yes, ma'am."

"That's more like it." Bea poured herself more coffee.

Kaylee looked at Reese. "Your favorite romance writer's daughter is getting married in our meadow Saturday evening. As she decided last night."

The three turned to the large picture window that looked over the back deck and yard to the meadow full of wildflowers and lavender. The early morning mist had burned off, and the sun's angle made subtle shadows in the softly swaying blooms.

"It'll be beautiful," Bea said. "What colors had Melanie picked for the wedding?"

"Don't know." Kaylee had never thought to ask. "You'll have to call Lorie."

"No thanks. Whatever she picks, it's bound to be echoed in the meadow. She's timed things well. In a few weeks there won't be nearly as much color."

"I'm charging for the meadow's use. Or rather, for our yard's use." Kaylee rinsed her coffee cup and put it in the dishwasher. "Did I tell you that, Grandma? I figure Lorelei can afford it."

Bea's smile was wide and warm. "Smart girl. Lorelei can

definitely afford whatever you told her and more. Now you and Reese go look at that boat. I'll see you at the shop later on."

They found the white, center console motor launch tied to a slip in a sea of other boats of all shapes and sizes. The name *KayBea* was printed across its back panel. How could she not love a boat named after her and her grandmother?

Yancy stood with them on the dock. "She's a good'un, she is. I remember when Ed bought her. Proud of her he was, and rightly so. Takes these waters like a champ no matter the weather."

"That's good to know." Kaylee studied the sleek and commanding craft, and it suddenly scared her to death. How was she supposed to drive something so powerful?

"You drive a car," Reese said, somehow reading her mind. "You can drive this."

"But if I mess up with a car, I don't fall into dark, cold, current-filled water with all kinds of creatures trying to nibble on me."

Yancy laughed as if she was kidding. "As long as you're floppin' around screamin' for help, they won't nibble." With a wave, he sauntered away.

"Thanks, Yancy," she called to his back. "That makes me feel much better." She turned to Reese. "But what if there's no one around to help? Nibble, nibble, nibble."

With a laugh at her absurdity Reese stepped onto the slightly rocking boat. He held out his hand to her. She picked up Bear and gratefully took it.

"Step there and then there," he instructed.

She did as told and stepped aboard. It was a minute before

she felt secure. When she set Bear down, he looked right, then left, then up at her, uncertain in this new environment that rocked slightly.

"Go explore," she encouraged. "This is our boat."

Bear took her up on the suggestion and began snuffling, nose to the deck. His tail waved like a furry metronome.

She watched him, her brave boy. If he could settle so quickly, so could she. "Do dogs go boating? Do they get seasick? I'll have to buy him a little life jacket. They do have them, right?"

"They do and most dogs love it." He examined the bells and whistles on the console. "They love the rush of the wind. I often see them sitting in the bow, ears flapping."

"Good." She didn't bother joining Reese at the console. She could study the dials and switches for hours and be no closer to solving their mysteries than she was right now. She'd learn about them all another day. For now she'd find something she could evaluate with some semblance of authority.

The boat's aesthetics. White hull. White interior. Gleaming chrome fittings. Keeping them shiny in the salty air would be a never-ending task. The deep blue upholstery was not yet faded by the sun and was in pretty good shape with only one seat showing any significant wear.

"Wonder what made this seat's upholstery come apart when the rest of the boat looks so good?" She poked at the heavy-duty fabric where the seam had split. Bear went up on his hind legs to examine the problem with her. With a little grunt he managed to get onto the low-slung seat.

Reese glanced over. "There are plenty of marine upholstery repair guys around."

Kaylee nodded and began moving around the boat. With the console in the middle, there was ample space to walk around the craft with large open areas in the front and back.

"You can sun in the front and fish in the back. Make everyone happy at the same time."

"That's fore and aft." Reese grinned at her. "You have to use the boating lingo."

"Right. No one would know what I meant if I said front and back."

A loud bell sounded and a powerful motor roared to life. Kaylee swung to see a large boat begin sliding from its slip. *Corzo Whale Watch* was emblazoned on its side. An open deck in the back—*aft*, Kaylee reminded herself—was filled with seats which in turn were filled with people. More people stood at the rails. Kaylee could see Roz Corzo standing on the dock watching the boat move into open water.

"Look, Bear. The lady who thinks you look like a rat."

Bear ignored her, his attention fixed on the seat he'd climbed onto.

Kaylee sat in the bow and lifted her face to the sun. "I haven't been on a boat for about twenty years."

"How is that possible?" Reese lifted a segment of the floor and peered into the darkness of the bilge beneath. "You lived in Seattle. Everyone in Seattle boats."

"Not me. Grandpa let me steer his when I was a kid, but what I liked best was sitting up front and taking the wind in my face. Sort of like you said the dogs sit, you know? Is there a boat-driving class I can take?"

"There is. The United States Power Squadrons offers online classes. You need to take them. Not only will you then know what you're doing, but you won't worry about being nibbled to death anymore."

"The old knowledge-is-power thing?"

"In this case, the boat is power. Knowledge is safety and security."

Kaylee liked safety and security. She also loved studying. Learning new things fascinated her, which was one reason she'd loved academia. "Have you taken the classes?"

"I have. I have my certification. You take the online classes for general knowledge, and I'll do the hands-on teaching specific to this launch."

She turned to him, her pulse giving a little blip, but he was busy peering over the back of the boat at the motor. "That'd be great." She hoped she sounded casual.

Bear gave a don't-ignore-me bark.

"What's wrong, Bear?" Kaylee rose and found him pawing at the fabric of the damaged seat. "Be careful. You'll make it worse."

She picked him up. He wiggled in her arms, struggling to get down. He gave another excited bark. Kaylee lowered him to the deck, and he promptly climbed onto the damaged seat. He began pawing at the bend between the seat and its back. He looked over his shoulder at her, then attacked the seat again.

Kaylee reached for him. "Stop it, Bear."

The normally obedient animal ignored her, pawing with increased frenzy. He pushed his nose against the bend.

"He's found something." Reese stood beside her, watching the dog. "Here." He leaned over, grabbed the seat, and flattened it into a chaise.

"How cool is that!" Kaylee imagined herself lying on the flattened seat, enjoying the sun. Bear barked triumphantly and put a paw over his treasure, which had been hidden in the crease of the bend. He looked at Kaylee with pride.

"What do you have there, guy?" Kaylee took hold of his collar and pulled him gently off his treasure. He wasn't happy with her move and struggled against her.

"Easy, boy. Easy, B—" Her mouth dropped open and she gaped at his find.

# 10

"That's a bullet casing." She looked at Reese. "Isn't it?" *A bullet casing! On Grandpa's boat!*

"Actually, it's the spent cartridge from a shotgun."

"Bullet casing. Spent cartridge. Tomato, tomahto."

"Never let anyone who knows guns hear you say that."

"You can shoot people with either one. That's all I need to know."

Reese looked at her strangely. "You can. You can shoot people with any kind of gun."

She pointed at the cartridge. "Someone shot my grandfather."

"That's a pretty big leap, Kaylee. All this cartridge proves is that someone dropped a spent cartridge that got caught in the bend of the seat. It's certainly not proof of what happened to your grandfather. It doesn't even prove the gun was discharged on the boat. It proves someone dropped a shell, period."

She made a face. "But it might be our first clue. It's the first indication of any kind about how he might have died."

Reese reached for the cartridge, and Bear let out a deep-throated growl. If he could have talked, he might've been saying, "Keep your grubby hands off my treasure! These teeth might be tiny, but they're very sharp!"

"Bear!" Kaylee put a hand on his back. "What are you doing?" She'd never heard him growl before.

Bear looked contrite, his tail down and his ears back, but he kept his eye on the spent cartridge and showed his teeth when Reese reached toward it again.

Kaylee stared at the empty shell. "Reese, we have to call the police. We have to tell them about this."

"Easy. Don't get too excited. We have no idea how long it's been here. Besides a shotgun isn't the typical weapon for shooting people."

"The police," she said stubbornly.

"Okay. It's better to err on the side of sharing it with them than to regret not doing so later. But I have a question. I thought it was his skiff that was found floating, not this boat. Isn't that part of the mystery?"

*The skiff!* Kaylee felt as if she had been struck in the chest. All the air fled her lungs, and she grabbed the seat back against the dizziness. How dumb could she be?

She watched Reese as he walked to the back of the boat and lifted one of the seat bottoms, revealing a storage compartment beneath. He rooted around and pulled out a piece of cloth. "This isn't too dirty." He held Bear back as he spread it over the cartridge. "Keep Bear away while I call the police."

"Maybe we shouldn't bother the police after all." She picked up the dog who complained loudly about being torn from his prize. "I mean, you're right about the skiff."

He pulled his phone free from the caddy attached to his belt. "Yeah, but maybe the skiff just broke away from its moorings and floated off. Did you ever think of that? Maybe this boat is the important one."

But Kaylee doubted it the more she thought about it. First her grandfather would never tie a boat loosely enough to break away and float off. Then, too, it was the skiff that was found floating, so it was the boat that held the secrets.

She wrapped her arms tightly around Bear who struggled and wiggled, his long body as supple as a cooked noodle.

"Stop it, Bear!"

He ignored her, making little yipping noises and squirming so much she had difficulty holding him.

"Here. Let me." Reese shoved his phone in his pocket and grabbed Bear around the middle with both hands. The dog was so surprised he went still and stopped barking. With one long reach, Reese deposited him on the dock.

Bear looked from Reese to Kaylee and back again, his eyes wide with shock. Kaylee was a bit surprised herself.

"Possible fingerprints," Reese explained. "The last thing you want is the dog messing with it any more than he already has."

*Of course.* She'd said herself it was a clue. She just hadn't gotten to wondering about prints yet, which was embarrassing given her work with the Seattle police department. She lifted the cloth and snapped a picture of the shell resting on the blue material. "Don't bullets have markings from manufacturers as well as ballistics marks?"

"Manufacturer's marks, yes, but ballistics? Maybe. Rifles cause markings, but shotguns are a tougher call. In any case, the police need a gun to compare them to. A deputy sheriff is on the way. It'll be up to him to figure it all out, but I've got to tell you that I don't think the shotgun that left that hull behind is the murder weapon."

Kaylee's shoulders sagged. They were finally going to solve the mystery and put Bea's mind at rest.

Bear ran up and down the dock, barking like a mad thing, finally crouching as if to jump back on the boat.

"No, Bear! No!" She held her hand out in a stop sign and said in an aside to Reese, "Doxies hate to miss out on the action, and they're possessive of their toys."

"Got to admire his persistence." Reese stared at the agitated dog. "No, Bear. No. Sit."

Bear stared at Reese, recognizing an order when he heard it. He sat and pouted silently, studying the gaping space between the dock and the boat. A gust of wind forced the boat away from the dock as far as its tether ropes would allow. Too far for a little dog to jump. With one last yip, Bear collapsed in a disconsolate heap, head on his paws.

"Good boy, Bear." But Kaylee knew that just because he was lying quietly for the moment didn't mean he'd given up on reclaiming what he considered his. "I'd better get out and clip him to his lead to make sure he doesn't throw himself at the boat and end up in the water."

Reese helped her out as he'd helped her aboard. She clipped on Bear's lead and crouched down beside him. "It's all right, buddy. It's all right." She sat cross-legged and drew him into her lap. She ran her hands down his back as she murmured to him. Slowly he calmed, finally relaxing against her legs. He gave a great sigh, but kept his eyes fixed on the seat even if he could no longer see his treasure.

"What's his problem?" The voice came from behind Kaylee.

She looked over her shoulder to see Roz Corzo standing a few feet away. "Hello, Roz. I saw your boat go out a while ago. Nice-looking craft."

Roz moved closer and grunted her thanks at the compliment. Today she wore a purple anorak that read Corzo Whale Watch, and her choppy hair was covered by a Mariners baseball cap. She gestured at Bear. "What's bothering the little rat dog?"

Kaylee slid her hands over Bear's ears to protect him from the tactless comment, but no worries. Bear wasn't listening. "He found a toy we won't let him have."

Roz studied the now sleepy Bear, worn out from all his exertions. "He's a determined little thing. I thought for a minute he was going to hurl himself at the boat and end up in the water. The big dogs can jump it—the labs and retrievers. Don't think a thing of it. They're water dogs. But this little guy? If the cold didn't get him . . . Does he even know how to swim? You got to get him a life vest if he's going to hang around the dock."

"It's on my list. I just found out I have a boat this morning."

"Ed's boat." Roz studied the craft from bow to stern and nodded her approval. "It's a good one, and he loved it. Liked to fish. Even told me about one of his favorite spots. Swore me to secrecy." She gave what passed for a smile. "Good spot. Had many a great dinner courtesy of Ed's generosity."

Kaylee smiled. "That sounds like Grandpa."

"Too bad he's gone. I saw him that last day you know."

"You mentioned that the day I met you at The Flower Patch."

"Yeah, I guess I did. Floppy hat and all. Quintessential Ed."

A crunch of gravel announced the arrival of the deputy sheriff. Kaylee rose, dislodging Bear who stood on sleep-wobbly legs beside her. Reese stepped off the boat to meet the officer who strode down the dock toward them.

"Nick." Reese stuck out his hand.

As they shook, Kaylee noted that Nick wasn't quite as tall as Reese. He had brown eyes and brown hair, a well-trimmed goatee, and he grinned at Reese in a way that let her know they were friends. "How you doing, Holt? Got something for me?"

"Maybe."

"Sounds interesting." Nick bobbed his head at Roz and gave her an engaging smile. "Mrs. Corzo. Nice to see you."

"Deputy." Roz flushed and almost smiled.

He turned to Kaylee, and his eyes widened in appreciation. He stuck out his hand. "Deputy Nick Durham."

"Kaylee Bleu."

"Ah. Bea Lyons's granddaughter. She's so happy you've come." He gave her a mischievous wink. "Me too."

Kaylee felt herself flush almost as much as Roz. "Thank you." She gave a little tug on her hand, and he released it immediately.

He pulled on his professional persona much as Lorie pulled on Lorelei. "So what's your concern? How can I help?" He looked at the three of them one at a time, ending at Reese.

"To understand everything, you need to meet Bear." Reese indicated the little dog.

Bear and Nick studied each other. "Cute little guy. I didn't know you had a dog, Holt."

"He's Kaylee's."

Nick grinned at her. "Lucky Bear."

Kaylee barely stopped herself from rolling her eyes. "He found what we called about on the boat."

"Let me show you," Reese said.

Reese and Nick stepped onto the boat while Kaylee stood on the dock with Bear and Roz. She watched Reese gesture as he explained about Bear's find, feeling slightly miffed. It was her boat, her dog, and her grandfather, and she was standing watching instead of being in the center of things. Nick glanced at her and read her expression. He winked again, then turned his attention back to Reese's explanation.

At least she thought he winked. It happened so quickly she wasn't sure.

The men climbed off the boat. Nick held out the cartridge, now in a plastic bag.

"Typical hunters' shot. High brass pellet shell." He looked at Kaylee. "Was your grandfather a hunter?"

"I don't know. You'll have to ask my grandmother."

"Duck hunting," Roz said. "He and my Richard and a couple of other men went every year."

Kaylee stared at the shell in Nick's hand as a deep disappointment spread through her. *Ducks.*

Nick slid the evidence pouch into his pocket. "Probably got caught in the seat the last time the men went out. They probably boated to old Mr. Jacobson's place, docked, and hunted the big pond in his meadow."

"That was Richard's favorite spot." Roz got the same faraway look in her eyes Bea sometimes got. "He and Ed went the fall before Richard died."

"I'm sorry, Kaylee, but I don't think this cartridge has anything to do with your grandfather's disappearance." Nick's eyes were kind. "But I'll do a thorough check."

"Thanks," Kaylee managed.

There was a moment of silence as Nick strode away. Kaylee stared at her feet while Roz made an indistinct mutter and followed. Reese patted her shoulder. "Sorry."

"Yeah."

He checked his watch. "I've got to get to the Ashford place. As far as the boat goes, I'll give Bea a full report, but I think it's in great shape."

"She'll be glad to hear that." Kaylee could hear the flatness in her voice. "And I've got to get to The Flower Patch."

By the time she got to the shop, Kaylee had control of her disappointment. After all, it wasn't as if she *wanted* her grandfather to have been shot. But the spike of hope that an answer might finally appear had been so exciting that the disappointment was proportionally difficult.

As she and Bear climbed the front steps of The Flower Patch, she practiced smiling until it felt almost real. She did not want her agitation to be visible to her grandmother. By the time she walked inside, she was pretty sure she could give Meryl Streep a run for her money.

As the bell over the door sounded, Bea looked up from the wedding consultation sitting area as if Kaylee were the storied Saint Bernard come to rescue the dying man in the snow. Her usually animated face had a forced, phony smile.

"Look, Melanie. Kaylee's here." Her voice wasn't actually shrill, but it was close. Her facial expression clearly said, "Help!"

Lorie Loblinski's daughter, absolutely beautiful with her long, red hair and emerald green eyes, spun gracefully to Kaylee, who had an immediate and visceral reaction. She who always liked everyone immediately didn't like Melanie, probably because of all that exceptional beauty and the expectation of homage that clearly went with it. That extraordinary magnificence wasn't natural. It couldn't be. It was too perfect. Hair dye—after all, Lorie had said her daughter was blond as a child—and tinted contacts. But the long, shapely legs were undeniably real, as was the amazing figure. *Jealousy is an ugly and petty emotion,* Kaylee reminded herself, to no avail.

Feeling tacky, grumpy, and underdressed in her dark jeans and cranberry top, Kaylee smiled with extra wattage. "Hello, Melanie."

"Hello, Kaylee." Melanie's voice was smoky and deep. "How nice you finally came to work. We've been waiting expectantly." The words slid from her mouth with a sweet smile.

Kaylee blinked. Had she just been dissed by an ill-mannered prom queen?

"Mellie, be nice."

For the first time Kaylee noticed Lorie sitting in a soft green slipper chair across from her daughter.

Beside Melanie on the love seat sat a pale young man with blond hair that waved nearly to his shoulders, like Errol Flynn in that old movie *The Adventures of Robin Hood.* Under brows so pale they disappeared into his skin, light blue eyes skimmed Kaylee with total disinterest.

"This is Ryan. The groom." Bea indicated the young man, who raised an eyebrow in greeting but otherwise moved not so much as a finger. Kaylee resisted an urge to put a hand over his heart to be certain it was beating.

"Nice to meet both of you." Kaylee smiled her best shopkeeper smile.

"We've been talking flowers for Mellie's wedding." Lorie spoke with the artificial brightness of someone trying to save a social situation from complete disintegration.

"Wonderful." Kaylee sat in the chair beside her grandmother, who had a book of sample photographs from weddings she had planned through the years spread on the coffee table before Melanie. "Have you seen anything in the book you like?"

"I want something original." Melanie flipped a page as if it weighed almost too much to move.

"Of course you do." Kaylee gestured to the beautiful arrangement on the page. "These pictures are just to give you ideas. The final outcome depends on taste, season, and pocketbook." Kaylee imagined that she almost sounded like she knew what she was talking about.

"Money's no object." Melanie's answer was quick, her assurance absolute. Kaylee noted Lorie's pained look, but she didn't object. Melanie continued without checking with her mother. "It's summer, so everything's available, and I'll let you know what I like."

Kaylee didn't doubt that for a moment. "It might be summer, but not everything is available, especially on such short notice."

Melanie frowned, that gorgeous face turning hard. Kaylee glanced at Ryan. Did he really want a wife who got mad every time something didn't go her way? He raised a finger and waggled it back and forth.

Melanie must have seen the movement out of the corner of her angry eyes. She looked at her lap for a minute, then up at Kaylee. Her expression was now calm and pleasant. "We'll just have to do the best we can, won't we?"

Lorie looked at Ryan with her mouth hanging open. Kaylee swallowed her own disbelief at the man's apparent power. "What colors will you be using for the wedding party?"

"Yellow. But no daisies. I don't want daisies." She flipped another page in the album.

"Not even colorful *Gerbera jamesonii*?"

Melanie's eyes went wide with confusion, and Bea shot her a look that said, "Katherine Leigh!" in that certain tone.

"Sorry." Kaylee gave a self-deprecating laugh, rose, and moved to the cooler. She pulled out four gerbera daisies in various colors. "I meant these."

"Um." Melanie looked at Ryan who blinked slowly, like a lizard, but gave no finger movements to guide his fiancée.

"Maybe we should wait to see what other blooms are available," Bea suggested. "Then you can decide which ones you like most."

"Melanie and Ryan have been engaged for a week." Lorie looked like she had swallowed something particularly tart. "I don't think they've had time to form an opinion about what they like and dislike."

Kaylee glanced at Ryan who gave that lizard blink again. She had the feeling that Ryan had an opinion on everything. He just couldn't be bothered to share it.

"Whirlwind romance. Right, babe?" Melanie rested her perfectly groomed hand with its beautifully manicured nails on Ryan's knee. "I don't know how I could have been so lucky."

Ryan managed to get his mouth to tip slightly.

Kaylee couldn't help glancing at Lorie, who at the moment had her eyes closed. Whether she was praying in her distress or merely blocking Ryan from her view, Kaylee couldn't tell. Both seemed appropriate given the circumstances.

"I suggest flowers of many summer hues." Bea indicated several photos of gorgeous bouquets. "Peonies, lavender, dahlias, snapdragons, sweet pea. Soft pinks, lavenders, creams, and rose. You can have spectacular flowers without a daisy in sight if that's what you want."

"A mix like that would look beautiful with the yellow." Kaylee put as much enthusiasm in her voice as possible.

"Just who is wearing yellow?" Lorie waved her hand around the room. "This is it, Mellie. You, Ryan, and me. And I'm not wearing yellow. It makes me look awful. I'm a cool-tones woman."

"Wear whatever you want, Mom." Melanie waved her mother's concern away as if it were as bothersome as a circling fly. She gave Kaylee a steely glare. "The flowers must be fresh."

Kaylee swallowed the offense. "Of course. We'll send an order to the Seattle Wholesale Growers Market today, and the flowers will come on the ferry tomorrow. As fresh as can be."

Melanie put her finger on a photo. "And I want the arbor with the tulle and the fairy lights just like this. And the flowering meadow. Won't that be lovely, Ry, babe?"

Ryan managed to look bored and disdainful at the same time as he rose. Melanie scrambled to her feet. He walked out and she followed.

Kaylee and Bea both looked at Lorie.

"I know! I know! It's awful. He's awful. But what can I do?" Lorie looked ready to cry.

Bea gave her a quick hug. "We'll make it as lovely as we can."

"Thanks." Her sigh was deep and from the heart. "You have

to love the irony. Here I am, a romance writer who espouses true love and happily ever after, but in this case, I'm hoping the divorce comes quickly." Steps dragging, she left.

"Poor Lorie." Bea watched her walk down the street.

Kaylee stuck the daisies back in the cooler. "I bet every guy Melanie's ever looked at has done everything she wanted. Ryan's different. He just about ignores her, and she's desperate for his attention. He's either as blah as he appears, or he's got her figured out. Did you see the finger waggle?"

"Lorie is one of the most irritating people I know." Bea walked toward the stairs. "But I wouldn't wish either Melanie or Ryan on her." She paused, looking thoughtful. "Of course, Melanie is her fault, isn't she?"

"I haven't the vaguest idea where a mother's training and an individual's personality converge or diverge. Beyond my pay grade. Come on. Show me how to do the ordering."

Two hours later Kaylee stood and stretched. "You can't move to Arizona. I'm never going to remember everything. I'm going to bring The Flower Patch to ruin."

Bea grinned. "You're doing fine, and don't forget Mary. She loves this place after all the responsibility that went with the dispatcher's job. Don't let her fool you. She knows a lot more than she lets on. She could run the shop with her eyes closed and do it as well as I do."

"I'll remember that." Kaylee blew out a breath. "The closer we get to you actually leaving, the scarier things get for me."

"You're a smart cookie, honey. You'll be fine."

Kaylee wished she had that certainty. "Once I get these flowers I just paid a small fortune for, I've got to make them look amazing. You plan on helping, right?"

"I will oversee your effort, offering suggestions as needed. But Melanie's wedding is your wedding."

Kaylee sighed. "As if I'm not overwhelmed here, I agreed to that side job with Reese."

"I'm so glad they're finally fixing the Ashfords' place up. It hurts knowing how it's been let go. Fortunately it's set back on that long drive and isn't seen from the road, so I haven't had to watch it decay."

"Want to run out with me and give me suggestions after Mary gets here?"

"Do I really want to see what it looks like?" She thought a moment. "Okay, Kaylee. I'll go with you, for Harry and Porter."

# 11

When Kaylee and Bea pulled into the drive, they found two vehicles, Reese's truck and a rental car.

Reese and another man emerged from the house as the women crossed the lawn.

"Well, look who's here!" Bea hurried forward. "Howie!"

"Bea!" The man rushed down the stairs and grabbed Kaylee's grandmother in a great big hug, lifting her off the ground. "It's been far too long."

"Howie, you look great! Just like your pictures, only better. I like the new hairstyle."

"My publisher hired a stylist and image consultant for me. Can you believe it? Made me, King of the Socially Inept, look cool. And please, no Howie. Bad for the new image, or so they tell me."

Kaylee watched, bemused. She knew she didn't know the man.

Bea stepped back, her smile wide. "Kaylee, meet Ward Meacham. Ward, this is my granddaughter, Katherine Leigh Bleu. Kaylee."

Ward Meacham? The great man himself? The vague something that had been gnawing at Kaylee's mind clicked into focus. She remembered her grandmother telling her about this would-be writer who had been trying so hard, coming every year to the Coterie with a new book he knew was "the one." He wanted Porter to read it and recommend him to his agent or publisher.

"It's just not going to happen for him, Kaylee," Bea had told her during one of their phone conversations. "It's really sad. He's a nice enough man if rather geeky. Porter says that if effort and desire were all it took, Howie'd be published many times over, but . . ."

"That's sad, sort of like someone who wants to be a great singer, but they don't have the voice."

"Ed says Porter will keep trying to help him."

"Of course he will. Mr. Ashford is a wonderful man."

"Porter says sometimes miracles happen."

Porter's kindness and Howie's persistence had certainly paid off. Ward Meacham had achieved all the success anyone could hope for. And here he was, right in front of her.

"Nice to meet you, Kaylee." His smile was charming, his handshake warm.

*Wait until the Petals hear about this.* "We weren't expecting you until Saturday, Mr. Meacham."

"About that. As I was just telling Reese, I'm not officially here yet. I snuck away from my keepers on the tour so I could have a day or two of quiet. Please don't tell anyone you saw me."

"Our lips are sealed," Bea assured him. "Where are you staying? I assume not Turtle Cove Inn with the other Coterie people."

"You know the old cabin at Bartram's Cove?"

"You mean Mermaid Cottage? But it's practically falling down."

"The new owner just finished fixing it up and is letting me be the first guest. It has a marvelous view over the Strait."

"It's fixed up?" Bea looked at Reese. "Your work?"

He looked like he'd been caught with his hand in the cookie jar. "Secret project. I've been working on it off and on for the last few months. I finished a couple of weeks ago, two weeks ahead of deadline."

"Of course you did. And who's the new owner?"

"Can't say."

"Can't or won't?"

Reese turned to the Ashford place as if he hadn't heard. "Do you think I should paint it? What if prospective buyers don't like green houses?"

"Good try changing the subject, but it won't work." Bea turned to Ward. "It's you, isn't it?"

Again that charming grin lit his face. "You are too clever."

Bea shrugged. "I try."

"You can't tell anyone." He surveyed the three of them. "I don't want company."

They gave assurances, and Kaylee felt she was included in a special group. She'd never joined a fan club before, but Ward's charisma was infectious and amazing. She would be happy to be president of his club.

Ward studied the shaggy house before them. "I just wanted to stop by for old times' sake. Porter was such a big help to me. I miss him."

"Don't we all." Bea sighed.

"And Ed." Ward put his arm around Bea's shoulders and gave her a brief hug. "So sad. He was a good man."

A few seconds of silence followed. Kaylee half-expected someone to say "amen" to signify the close of the special moment.

"I've got to get going." Ward was suddenly all business. "Remember. I'm counting on you to keep my secret." With a wave, he climbed in his car and drove away.

"Wow." Kaylee stared after him.

"This is all wrong." Bea stood in the middle of Porter Ashford's office. "It's neat."

"Exactly my reaction." Kaylee felt vindicated.

"Harry used to despair of this room. She wouldn't even attempt to clean it. Porter used to say he knew where everything was and that he thought better when the place looked 'lived in.'" Bea walked to the collection of Porter's titles and ran a hand over the books. She turned and surveyed the immaculate room again. "Even Harry would hate it like this. I wonder who . . ."

"Don't feel bad, Grandma. Jules probably hired someone to clean without telling anyone, even Isaac and Ursula. You know he's not good at understanding others' feelings."

"You're probably right. He has all the social skills of a slug. It never computed for him that cleaning up after Porter would help Ed and me in our grief. Now where did you discover that thumb drive yesterday?"

Kaylee had been so disappointed last night when she went to read what was on the thumb drive and realized she'd left her laptop at the shop. She'd had to settle for reading the pages she'd pulled from the wastebasket. What fascinated her most was seeing the corrections Porter had made on them. To her the original sentences and word choices looked fine, but his changes made them richer, deeper, and more beautiful. More alive.

It was sort of like looking at a work of art and wondering how the artist knew to use that color there and only so much of it, making the work striking instead of merely competent. Or when to use a specific technique to bring the painting from fine to extraordinary. Instead of paints, Porter's medium had been words. He painted a picture by calling the girl *lovely* instead of merely *pretty*. He painted emotion with words like *anguished* and *enraged* rather than *sad* and *mad*.

*The mystery of creativity*, she thought.

As a scientist her mind worked differently—logically, factually. She dealt with proofs and established patterns, with absolutes proven by scientific method. In taxonomy she and all the others in her field followed the Linnaeus method, a system of rules that standardized plants into a hierarchy: kingdom, phylum, class, order, family, genus, species. "King Phillip Came Over From Germany Saturday," her high school biology teacher used to say. Kaylee was used to a place for everything and everything in its place.

She was going to have to start thinking artistically if she was to be a florist who did more than re-create someone else's arrangement. She didn't want to be like the painters who made careers of copying the masters. She wanted to be creative, as creative as her grandmother or Porter or Ward Meacham. As creative as Reese with his excellent carpentry skills.

But wanting and being were two different things. The old feelings of inadequacy had made for a restless night.

"The thumb drive, Katherine Leigh," Bea repeated. "Where did you find it?"

"Right. Over here." Kaylee pulled out *They Came Alone*. "It was behind this book."

Bea peered into the space. "Strange. Is there anything else behind the other books?"

Kaylee blinked. She'd never thought of that. She began pulling books, taking care to keep them in order as she placed them on the desk. Soon there was a long shelf holding nothing but dust.

Bea shrugged. "It was just a thought."

As they began replacing the books, Reese walked into the room. He nodded toward the shelf. "No other hidden treasures?"

"None." Kaylee arranged five paperback versions of *They Came Alone*, all with Ondor and Violine flying across the cover, all stylistically different. "This is my favorite of his titles."

"Mine too." Reese pointed to the cover done dramatically in red, black, and white. "I had that one."

Kaylee held up a cover done in softer colors, the dragons flying over lush countryside. "This was the one I had."

Bea straightened the original hardback. "It's hard to believe this was first published so long ago."

Kaylee did some quick figuring. "Twenty-six, twenty-seven years ago. I was about twelve when I got the dragon salt and pepper shakers."

Bea held out a paperback with a castle and a knight on the cover. "His first book. *Over There*. We all hated the title. It made us want to sing that World War I song, but as a new writer, Porter had no power to override the editors and get it changed. Of course his wasn't any better. *The Knight Beneath the Tree*."

"Ouch." Kaylee laughed.

"But the tree was magical, and the knight, the vanquisher of Eveal, was the only one who could sit safely beneath it." Reese was once again studying the water spot in the ceiling as he spoke. "I've read everything Porter wrote since *Over There*."

Bea smiled as her eyes went vague with memory. "We had such a celebration when it was released, Harry and Porter, Ed and me. That started the tradition of the four of us going out for a celebratory dinner after each release. We ate a lot of those meals through the years, though none was quite as happy an occasion as that first. Porter reaching his dream." She laughed. "The next-best one was the day Porter decided he could quit his job as a teacher and write full time."

Kaylee tucked the last book back on the shelf. "*They Came Alone* is still my favorite."

Bea pulled her glasses off and let them dangle by the chain around her neck. "Ed loved that book too, but he thought the one Porter was working on when he died was his best."

"The unknown book that Jules got?" Kaylee wandered over to stare out the front window at the wild shrubs she had to tame.

"I've wondered for years what happened to that book." Bea began pulling open desk drawers, looking disgusted at their neatness. "I think Ed's biggest frustration about not being allowed into the house after Porter's death was his inability to get hold of that book and get it to Porter's agent." She glanced around the room again. "Too neat!"

Reese glanced at Bea over his shoulder. "Kaylee said the same thing. So did Ward."

"They'd know," Bea said. "They spent a lot of time here with Porter."

Reese abandoned his study of the water spot and leaned a hip against the desk. "Ward was standing out front when I pulled up, just studying the house. He introduced himself and explained why he was here, sort of a Porter Ashford pilgrimage. When he realized I was coming inside to work, he asked if he could come in with me. He went straight to the office."

The rattle of a vehicle outside made Reese turn and look. "The plumber's finally here to check the upstairs leak. Excuse me."

Bea gave one last look around the room. "I am sometimes amazed at how much my life has changed, and this room brings it home with all the subtlety of a punch to the heart. Harry and Porter gone. Ed gone." She sighed. "But it was worth it to know and love them for the years that I could. Be sure you really live, Katherine Leigh. When you get to my age, how sad it would be if you had no losses to mourn."

With that, she left the room and the house.

With mounting excitement Kaylee climbed into bed, plumped the pillows behind her, and slipped the thumb drive into the

USB port on her laptop. The box that appeared on her screen told her there was one document—Version 5.

She double clicked, and Version 5 opened to Chapter One. In the header were the name *Porter Ashford* and the page number. She quickly copied the file to her laptop and began to read.

*Riley Morgan did not know what to believe.*

Soon Kaylee was lost in Riley's life, entranced by the story of his family and their trials and triumphs during World War II. It was a story told in the pattern of *To Kill a Mockingbird* or *Cold Sassy Tree*—a story told from the point of view of a child or young teen but written for adults. Riley struggled to balance family problems with international catastrophe while trying to determine who he was. At fourteen, too young to fight but old enough to feel fear and loss, Riley faced each day with curiosity and uncertainty. His inability to participate in the war effort—like his older brothers and father off fighting and his mother in the defense plant making fighters and bombers—ate at him. He found a common struggler in his grandfather who was too old and ill to be anything but an air-raid warden. Together they worked to hold their fragmented family together as Riley asked life's hard questions: *What is loyalty? What is responsibility? What is family? Where is God?*

And was Mrs. Germaine, the daughter of his grandfather's girlfriend, the saboteur at the plant? "She always has real stockings," Riley's mother said, while she and her friends had to paint their stockings on and draw the seam line up the back of their legs with an eyebrow pencil.

Version 5 was like nothing Porter had written before. No castles or knights, no princes or princesses, no dragons or kingdoms. Just a boy like every other boy, and yet like no other boy. The book crackled with life and humor as well as deep emotion. Kaylee, non-authority that she was, knew she held a masterpiece in her hands.

Her eyelids grew heavy in spite of her concern for Riley's brother, now missing in action. She glanced at the clock. One thirty. She'd been reading for almost four hours, and she had to get some sleep. Tomorrow would be preparations for Melanie's wedding, as the flowers her agent had acquired would arrive on the early ferry. And there was the prep for the book signing. She and her grandmother had promised not only flowers, but a cheese board and crackers.

Sleep. She must sleep.

But first she had a mystery of her own to solve. She grabbed the pages she'd pulled from the wastebasket. She checked page numbers and looked for corresponding numbers in the manuscript. They didn't match page for page, but they matched with the words of the corrections added. She must be holding Version 4 in her hands as she read Version 5 on the laptop.

And Porter's name was in the header of Version 5.

She slid the pages into the red folder she'd purloined from his office, disconnected the thumb drive from her laptop, and tucked it in the folder too. She laid it on the far side of the big bed beside her laptop. There was no question in her mind—she'd found Jules's unknown manuscript.

And it was wonderful!

# 12

Coffee in hand to try and wake herself, Kaylee met the early ferry to receive the flowers that had been sent. She checked the order against the invoice to be sure everything was there, transported the flowers to The Flower Patch and refrigerated them. They were beautiful blooms, a soft yet rich rainbow of color. They'd make the wedding beautiful. The flowers for the signing were there too: salmon gerberas, white daisies, and sprigs of lavender.

Before she could begin work on the flowers, Kaylee went with her grandmother to the gourmet boutiques in Eastsound for cheeses and crackers. They loaded the bags in the Escape and drove to Wildflower Cottage to store everything.

Finally shortly after ten, tucked in her office at The Flower Patch with Bear snoozing at her feet, Kaylee had time to text Reese for Isaac Ashford's contact information. She had actually had her phone in her hand last night, ready to call Isaac with the news of what she'd found. Then she'd glanced at the clock again. She could not call in the middle of the night. Middle-of-the-night calls were about life-and-death situations. He'd waited seven years for the information she had, so what would a few more hours matter? But excitement rippled through her at the thought of the call. How often would she get the chance to tell someone she had solved a mystery for him?

"Isaac? This is Kaylee Bleu, Bea and Ed Lyons's granddaughter."

She realized after she spoke that she'd called Isaac by his first name for the first time. The last time she'd talked with him, she'd been young and he'd been Mr. Ashford—which had been confusing when his father and his brother were also in the room. Say "Mr. Ashford" and three men said, "Yes?"

"Hello!" Isaac sounded much as Kaylee remembered. "This is a nice surprise. How are you?"

At his genial welcome, her nerves calmed. "Doing well, thanks. I'm living on Orcas now. I've bought my grandmother's shop and house."

"Is Bea all right?" His voice grew sharp with concern.

"She's fine," Kaylee assured him. "Just retiring and moving to Arizona to live with her twin sister."

Isaac laughed. "Talk about a change of scenery. Washington evergreens for Arizona cacti. Water everywhere for hot and arid desert."

Kaylee hummed agreement. "I know."

Kaylee could feel Isaac's curiosity as he waited for her to explain the reason for the call. The moment of the big reveal was at hand. Kaylee rubbed a damp palm on her jeans. "I have news for you." She took a deep breath and blurted, "I've found your father's missing manuscript."

There was a moment of shocked silence. "You're kidding!"

Like she'd kid about something like this.

"But where? How?"

"I was at your dad's to help prepare the place for sale and—" She told him about finding the pages and the thumb drive. "I started reading the manuscript last night. Isaac, it's wonderful! Very different from your dad's usual work, but wonderful."

"I can't believe it. After all this time." Isaac started to laugh. "Wait until Jules hears."

"He finally gets his book."

"But he doesn't. That's the funny part."

Kaylee leaned back in her desk chair. "I don't understand."

"You know he's been holding up settlement of the estate for years with his challenges."

"I do."

"Just last week we—that's Ursula and I—we each gave him a book of ours so things could finally be settled. I gave him *Not By Might*, one of Dad's evergreens."

"Oh, Radland and Mercelle and the magic scepter."

"Right. And Ursula gave him *Never-Ending Night*."

Kaylee frowned. "I'm not familiar with that one."

"It's a novella. It's not as well-known as some of Dad's other titles, but it's being cast for a movie as we speak. An A-list director is already signed."

Kaylee imagined Jules rubbing his hands together with glee at what his stubbornness had won him. Bettina undoubtedly smirked nearby, planning everything she would buy with their sudden windfall. "So who gets Version 5?"

"My sister and I will split it."

"Do you have it in writing that he traded Version 5 away? Because you're going to laugh all the way to the bank, believe me. Granted I'm only about halfway through the book, but I love it. You're going to love it. *Everyone's* going to love it." Maybe a little hyperbole, but not much.

Isaac laughed again. "I love your enthusiasm. I can't wait to read it. As to Jules, he made us put everything in writing, signed before witnesses, notarized, and every other legal thing he could think of. *Not By Might* and *Never-Ending Night* are completely his, as is any income they generate. We made sure the unknown book was legally ours, as was any income it generates, even though we never anticipated it being found. We did it more on a tit-for-tat basis, if you know what I mean."

Crabby, petty Jules. His greedy, me-first attitude was about to cause him to miss out on a fortune.

"What should I do with the book?" Kaylee asked. "Should I mail you the thumb drive?"

Silence hung in the air as Isaac thought. "Has anyone seen the book besides you?" he finally asked.

"No. I haven't even shown my grandmother."

"Okay, that's good. Don't say anything to anyone. I want your word. There might be a lot of money involved here if it really is Dad's book. He's become more popular than ever with the recent surge in fantasy sales."

"I have to tell you Reese Holt knows about the thumb drive."

"But not what's on it?"

"Not what's on it."

"Please keep it that way. I need to figure out how to prove it's Dad's work, especially since you say it's so different."

"His name is in the header."

"Mmm."

She felt his uncertainty and understood. "But anyone could type his name, like his son who wanted to profit from his father's reputation."

"Exactly. It probably is his, but—"

"We found it in his house. Rather Reese found it." She couldn't help grinning as she gave credit where it was due. *If we're going to be accurate,* he'd said, *I found it.* "He can verify that it was hidden behind your dad's books or had fallen there."

"That's good. Reese has nothing to gain here."

"And he knows about the papers too. He was with me when I found them."

"What papers?"

Kaylee sat up straight as the importance of the papers dawned on her. "We found papers in the wastebasket under the desk in the office. They're pages from the book with handwritten corrections in the margins and between the lines.

You know the way your father always worked."

Isaac grunted. "Saw it many times."

"It's his writing on those pages. I recognized it."

"And you still have these pages?"

"I do."

"And they match pages in Version 5, which has Dad's name on it?"

"They do." Kaylee could feel his excitement.

"That's our provenance. Dad never went page by page on other people's work. He just read it and gave general feedback."

And these key papers had been lying in that black wastebasket under the desk for seven years with no one the wiser. It was enough to make her head spin.

"Don't let anything happen to those papers, Kaylee. If I was adamant about secrecy before, I'm even more so now. Remember, you gave me your word."

"I understand. I'll make sure they're well cared for." Mentally she saw them lying on her bed where anyone could find them. She swallowed. "Do you want me to mail them to you? And the thumb drive?"

"I don't like the idea of them leaving your hands until you put them in mine. I think I'll come to Orcas Sunday."

So she was responsible for two and a half days. She swallowed again. "It'll be good to see you. Grandma will love it."

"Right. Until Sunday." And he was gone.

Kaylee slid her phone into her pocket. Where could she put that red folder to make certain its contents were safe? Her eyes fell on the file cabinet in the corner of the office. She smiled. She'd hide it in plain sight. Nobody would think to look there.

She stopped at the door to the workroom where her grandmother was busy stripping stems. She sat on a high stool, the sharp knife in her hands making leaves fly. The floor was green with discards.

"I have to run home for a minute."

"What for? I could use your help."

"I know. I'll be back as soon as possible. Can I bring you anything?"

"Just you for the rest of your day."

"Got it." She looked at Bear, who looked back hopefully. "Stay with Grandma, buddy. I won't be long."

With a disgruntled look into the workroom and its chaos, he wandered back to the office with his little dog bed in the corner.

Downstairs, Kaylee was reaching for the shop door when it burst open and a distraught Lorie Loblinski practically fell into the room. The tinkling of the bell over the door was lost in her frustrated scream.

Mary was helping a lady decide which of the lovely grapevine wreaths she would buy, and they both looked up in a combination of surprise and concern. Kaylee jumped back to avoid being run over.

"Where's your grandmother?" Lorie looked feverish.

"In the workroom upstairs. Are you all right?"

"No." Lorie grabbed Kaylee's hand and dragged her toward the workroom.

Kaylee smiled over Lorie's shoulder at the grapevine lady, who was edging her way to the door empty-handed.

"Please come again," Kaylee called as the woman pulled the door open and fled.

"Lorie!" Mary snapped, hands on hips. "You just cost me a sale. What is the matter with you?"

Lorie looked at her, wild-eyed. "Do you need to ask?"

*Of course.* "Melanie?" Kaylee ventured.

"Melanie," Lorie confirmed.

"What is all this?" Bea demanded as she came into the main room.

"Melanie and her friends." Lorie leaned against the register counter as if for support. "Five of them showed up on the ferry this morning."

Kaylee frowned. "And this is bad? It'll be nice for her to have them at the wedding."

"Not *at* the wedding. *In* the wedding."

"Like bridesmaids?"

"Bridesmaids. They each arrived carrying a yellow dress."

"Bridesmaids." Kaylee turned cold. "Bouquets." She turned in panic to her grandmother. "We didn't order enough for six bouquets, did we?"

Bea looked thoughtful rather than alarmed. "We did not. Melanie never mentioned bridesmaids." She pointed at Kaylee. "Time to improvise. The meadows behind our house and the Ashfords'. Look for lavender, poppies, paintbrush, lupines, black-eyed Susans, and any other kind of daisy."

"She doesn't want daisies," Lorie protested.

Bea's expression grew fierce. "She's getting what she gets. Five bouquets she neglected to mention? She's lucky those girls won't be carrying air."

"You're right." Lorie held out a placating hand. "Whatever you can do."

Bea turned to Mary. "You hit the Petals' gardens. Peonies, all kinds and shades, I don't care. Ranunculus and coreopsis. Zinnias and snapdragons if you can find any this early. And if you see hydrangeas, a bonanza. I don't care what color. With yellow dresses we can use all kinds of colors. Any and all interesting greens. Lots of everything. Got it?"

Mary and Kaylee nodded. Mary looked determined, and Kaylee was impressed by her grandmother's ability to so quickly see a solution to their dilemma.

"Go!" Bea shooed them to the door. "Lorie, you're on the

register in case anyone comes shopping."

"But—" Lorie sputtered. Bea just glared at her. "Yes, ma'am."

With a "that's more like it" nod, Bea headed back to the workroom.

Kaylee's first stop was Wildflower Cottage. She raced into the house for the red folder whose contents might be worth a fortune. She grabbed it from where it lay on her bed and raced back out. She tossed it on the car seat and slammed the door. She hit the lock button on her key fob.

She hadn't taken a step before the bright red splash on the passenger seat brought her up short. *Too obvious.* Even though no one but she and Reese knew what was in that folder and he didn't know its significance or its location, it seemed to scream, "Take me! I'm valuable!"

She pulled the door open and grabbed the folder. She bent and slid it under the passenger seat, pushing it back far enough that it wasn't visible. This time when she closed and locked the door, she felt much better.

She grabbed one of the buckets she'd brought with her and went to the spigot at the side of the house. She filled the bucket and carried it to the car, trying not to slosh out all the water she'd just put in. When she set the bucket on the floor behind the driver's seat, she realized she'd have to wedge it in place somehow. The last thing she wanted was for the bucket to go over when she turned a corner or went around a curve. Water all over the place would be the least of it. Broken stems and squashed flowers wouldn't help with all those bouquets, and water would ruin the fortune under the passenger seat. She raced to the patio and grabbed the chair pillows. She stuffed them all around the bucket.

She flipped the lock once again and headed for the meadow. Time blurred as she snipped and stripped and swatted at bugs. She walked to the back of the meadow to work so the view from the house and yard would still be flower-filled for the wedding. As she strode through the high grasses and flowers, insects rose in clouds. It hadn't occurred to her to use bug spray. Thankfully she had on jeans and a long-sleeved shirt, but that didn't keep them out of her mouth, nose, and eyes.

"You'd better appreciate my sacrifice, Melanie Loblinski," she muttered with venom after a particularly nasty bite on her neck. Like that would ever happen.

She persevered, putting the cut flowers in the large, yellow plastic pail she was carrying. When she finally waded back to the yard, she was hot, sweaty, bug-bitten, and her back hurt from all the bending, but her pail was full of beautiful, fragrant flowers. She transferred them carefully to the bucket of water, checked that the folder was still in its hiding place, and went inside to splash cool water on her face and neck. She pulled a bottle of cold water from the fridge and drank. She grabbed another to drink after her next meadow.

She drove to the Ashford place and repeated the drill with the bucket and pillows she'd brought from home, then sprayed herself liberally with bug spray she'd found in her grandmother's hall closet. This time she didn't care if she cut flowers close to the house. There would be no wedding here, and buyers wouldn't buy or not buy the property depending on the flowers they could see in the meadow.

Yellow pail in hand, she waded again into the tangle of flowers and grasses. Again clouds of insects rose with every step, but those not blown away by the breeze turned up their little bug noses at her scent. If she hadn't been so tired and sore, she might have had fun.

She had scarcely begun her snipping and stripping when a black pickup pulled into the drive and parked beside her Escape. Reese climbed out, waved, and walked to the edge of the yard.

Today his flannel shirt was brown and tan, and his T-shirt was deep brown. His Dodgers cap was pulled low to shade his eyes from the sun.

"Whatcha doing?" he called.

*Whatcha doing?* She stared at him. She was standing in the middle of the meadow with a pail of flowers in one hand and a pair of shears in the other, and he was asking what she was doing? Then she realized he couldn't see the pail, so she lifted it up. "Flowers for Melanie Loblinski's wedding tomorrow."

"Right. Bea called me to help with the setup. A trellis or some such thing?"

"For the bride and groom to stand under."

Kaylee bent to snip a *Lupinus latifolius*. By the time she straightened with the spiky blue lupine in her hand, Reese was halfway to the house. Just as well. She didn't have time to stand around and talk.

Her pail was nearly full when a patrol car sped into the driveway and skidded to a halt, gravel flying. As she stared, Deputy Nick Durham jumped out and sprinted toward the house.

# 13

$W$*hat in the world?* She pushed her way through the meadow and scrambled over the fence that set it off from the yard. She raced to the front porch, her pail bumping her legs.

"Reese!" She ran up the steps. "What's wrong?" She got no answer.

A second car roared into the drive and squealed to a stop behind the sheriff's department vehicle. Kaylee paused on the porch and saw Ward Meacham climb out.

He hurried toward her. "Is everything all right?"

"I don't know." She dropped the pail beside the door and rushed inside. Ward sprinted up the steps, and entered the house on her heels.

They screeched to a halt in the front hall where they found Reese and Nick standing and talking calmly.

Kaylee looked from one to the other, her heart racing with a combination curiosity and concern. "What's wrong? Is someone hurt?"

The men glanced at each other. Apparently Reese was silently elected spokesman. "Someone broke into the house. I called and reported it, and Nick responded to the call."

"Someone broke in?" She looked around the hall. Nothing seemed out of place. She looked at the front door soon to be painted white. It didn't seem damaged.

"Why are you here, Kaylee?" Nick asked.

She blinked. Who cared why she was here? She wanted to know what happened. "I was picking flowers in the meadow." She could see he needed more. "For a wedding tomorrow. They're in a bucket on the porch."

"That's where she was when I got here," Reese said. "She's also helping me prepare this property for sale."

"It's finally going on the market?" Nick seemed surprised.

"Just happened." Reese pulled off his cap and slapped it against his leg. "I've been hired to do the inside work, and I've hired Kaylee to do the outside. The gardens and all, you know."

"Curb appeal," Kaylee offered.

Nick grunted and turned to Ward. "What brings you here, sir?"

They all turned to Ward, who was staring at the floor at the foot of the stairs. He looked stricken.

"Are you all right?" Kaylee took a step toward him.

He shook himself and forced a smile. "Bad memories."

Kaylee sucked in a breath. Her eyes fixed on the spot where Ward had been staring. She could imagine Porter sprawled there, and knew how hard this must be for the man who had discovered him. She tore her eyes away from the floor and fixed them on the author's face. "Is that where . . .?"

Ward took a deep breath and focused on Nick. "You passed me going too fast for normal circumstances. In my rearview mirror I saw you turn in here, so I turned around in the first drive I came to and followed you. I was afraid something awful had happened here again. Porter was my mentor and a good friend. I was the one who found him here when he died."

Nick looked unimpressed, though he nodded politely. "Can you give me your name and address?"

Kaylee noted Ward seemed slightly taken aback that Nick didn't recognize him, and his brow furrowed when he gave his name, and Nick still showed no reaction.

Kaylee could stand the suspense no longer. "So how do you know someone broke in?"

Nick gestured to the office. She walked to the door and

looked in. Her heart dropped, and she grabbed the doorjamb for support. "Who would do this?"

All the books were on the floor, many with their backs broken and their pages torn or bent. The chair before the big window, the one Porter always sat in, was slashed, its innards pulled out and thrown around the room. "His chair!" For some reason seeing it so disfigured hit Kaylee hard. She hurried toward it, reaching for some of its stuffing as if she could put it back.

"Don't touch anything, Kaylee." Nick's voice was loud and authoritative.

"Sure. Right. Of course." She knew that. She watched television. *Don't contaminate the crime scene. Basic crime investigation 101.* She drew her hand back and tucked it in her jeans pocket, hoping no one saw that it was shaking.

She took a step away from the chair and was aware for the first time of the grit under foot. "The *Saintpaulia ionantha*! Someone killed it!" She saw the dead plant lying under what was left of Porter's chair. Someone had pulled the African violet from the wastebasket in the knee well and torn it from the pot. The dirt had been flung around the room and ground into the rug, the plant tossed to land where it might.

"Kaylee." Reese put a hand on her shoulder. "It was dead long ago."

She swallowed the sour taste in her throat. "I know. I'm being stupid."

"You've had a shock."

"I loved Mr. Ashford. He was like a second grandfather when I was a kid. It hurts that someone could be so mean to him even after he's gone."

Nick had been studying the room and taking pictures with his phone. "Can you tell if anything is missing in here?" He looked first at Kaylee, then Reese, then Ward.

Ward shrugged helplessly. "I haven't been here for years, not since Porter's death."

As he spoke, Kaylee spun to the desk. She'd been so focused on the chair and the plant she hadn't taken in the chaos in that area—and what that chaos might mean.

The box of red folders that she'd taken one from had been dumped, and the folders flowed across the floor like a meandering crimson stream. Pens and pencils, once neatly placed in a mug, lay scattered on the desk and floor. The mug that had held them lay in the knee well, a new chip in its rim. The little compartmentalized tray that held paper clips and other office supplies was dumped on the desk. The ergonomic chair lay on its side, its seat cushion a victim of the same slashing as Porter's comfy chair.

The drawer in the center of the desk hung open and empty.

"The folder's gone." Reese had turned pale.

"What folder?" Nick asked.

"The one that held some manuscript pages and a thumb drive."

"We found them." Kaylee waved vaguely toward the bookcase, her mind racing. All the mess was to cover for the search for that folder. She was sure of it.

"We put them in one of those red folders and left them right there." He pointed at the empty drawer.

"What pages did you find? And what thumb drive? Where did you find them?" Nick bombarded them with questions.

"I found the pages in the wastebasket under the desk." Kaylee indicated the basket still undisturbed in the back of the knee well.

Ward bent and looked. "You can't see that back there, can you? Black blending with the shadows."

"That's undoubtedly why the papers were still there." Kaylee rubbed her forehead, trying to massage away her headache.

"And I found the thumb drive behind *They Came Alone.*" Seeing Nick's blank look, Reese clarified. "One of Porter's books. On this shelf." He indicated the now empty space.

"And you put them in the desk drawer?"

"Until I could tell one of his children." Reese looked pained. "We thought they'd be safe there."

Nick snapped a couple of pictures of the drawer and the empty shelf. "And these pages are important? The drive had important stuff on it?"

"I don't know," Reese said. "Kaylee thought they might be a long-lost book of Porter's, but we didn't think it was right to read what wasn't ours."

Kaylee hoped the burn of embarrassment didn't show in her overly red cheeks. She'd read much of that private material and planned to read the rest.

Reese slapped his hat back on his head. "And now it looks like they're lost again."

But they weren't lost, and all because she had followed her instincts. "I guess it's a good thing—"

She became aware of the three men watching her, and she ground to a halt as Isaac's words played in her mind.

*"Has anyone seen the book besides you?"*

*"No. I haven't even shown my grandmother."*

*"Okay, that's good. Don't say anything to anyone. I want your word."*

And she'd given it. She had promised she would tell no one. She would protect everything until Isaac arrived Sunday and she handed it all to him. She looked at Reese, Ward, and Nick. Trustworthy men all, but she'd given her word.

"It's a good thing what?" Nick asked.

She swallowed, hoping she was making the right choice. Withholding information from the police was not a lawful thing, but she felt she had no choice. And it was only for two days. "It's a good thing Mr. Ashford can't see this mess. It would upset him immensely. It upsets me."

"Yeah, I'm sure it does," agreed Nick. "Now let's check the rest of the house."

"There were some things upset in other rooms." Kaylee slit the end of a hydrangea stem and plunged it in fresh water. "You could tell someone looked under the beds and under the mattresses." But no one knew to look under her passenger seat where the folder still lay. "Drawers weren't pushed shut, and things in them were in disarray. Clothes were lying on the floor in the closet."

"Clothes?" Bea looked shocked. "There are still clothes in the closet after seven years?"

The two sat in the workroom. Bea made the floral pieces for the big event at Between the Lines in the morning while Kaylee prepped blooms for the wedding bouquets and arrangements. Mary was out front tending to customers.

"Remember, Grandma, no one has been allowed in the house before, thanks to Jules." Kaylee looked at the buckets of blooms. "Do you think we have enough for you to make little corsages or boutonnieres for the authors?"

"Between your haul and Mary's, we're loaded. Let's do it." And in no time Bea had created three small corsages and three boutonnieres.

"You are amazing!"

Bea looked pleased as she refrigerated the finished work for the signing. "Now for the wedding altar flowers."

Kaylee pictured the base of their yard and the white wooden fence. "What do you set arrangements on for an affair like Melanie's where there is no altar?"

"We've got two pairs of three white wooden tables of different heights, sort of like nice lecterns but with flat tops instead of slanted. With them we can give a bride as many or as few flowers as she wants, no matter the setting. They look very nice with the white arbor and fairy lights."

"How many tables does Melanie want?"

"Lorie's coming in to finalize things, and she'll tell us." Bea looked at her watch. "She should be here momentarily."

Mary walked into the workroom. "Look who I found."

Lorie walked in wearing a black top and slacks. Over them she wore a stylish knee-length lightweight coat of many colors that would have made Joseph of the Bible story jealous. Somehow the wild swirls looked good on her despite their busyness.

Bea's eyes widened. "That's some coat."

"No wisecracks. I love it, it cost a fortune, and I threw it in my luggage at the last minute, never really expecting to wear it. Thank heavens I did. I need its armor for the bridesmaids' tea this afternoon and tonight's rehearsal dinner."

"Where are you going for the tea?" Kaylee asked.

"Lila's Tea House in Eastsound, and we're doing dinner at The Ideal Meal over on Sea Cliff."

"Did Reese have anything to do with that choice?" Bea grinned. "It's the best steak and seafood place in town."

"I think he did suggest it."

Kaylee stood and offered Lorie her stool. Lorie sank gracefully onto it. "Thanks. I've had a rough day."

"Melanie?"

"And her five friends. And Ryan the Loser. The girls never stop talking and Ryan never starts. He just sits there, quirking an eyebrow or moving a finger, and Mellie does whatever he wants. What I can't figure out is how she knows his code. Did he sit her down and say, 'When I move my finger to the left, I want you to sit, and when I move it to the right, I want you to stop talking.' I just don't get it."

Without looking up, Bea snipped greens. "Love is a complicated thing, Lorie. It's different for each couple. You should know. You write about it all the time."

"But I write about it like we all wish it was. Handsome, manly heroes who support and accept the lovely heroine, who actually talk to her, and of course, they live happily ever after."

Kaylee put a green-stained hand over her heart. "You mean it isn't really like that? I've been looking for an unachievable ideal? No wonder I'm still single."

"It was pretty much like that for your grandpa and me," Bea said. "Not perfect, but wonderful. Definitely happy ever after."

"Didn't work so well for me in real life." Lorie managed a smile. "Still not quite sure what went wrong."

Bea looked at her in surprise. "You still love him."

Lorie shrugged, and things were quiet for a few minutes, the only sounds the rustle of leaves and the snipping of stems. Lorie sat with her eyes closed, and Kaylee wondered if she was thinking of her Dennis or just savoring the quiet.

"This silence is wonderful," Lorie said, and Kaylee had her answer. "I'm not used to noise, you know. I work alone. I live alone. This wedding drama is making me crazy. Things were quiet for a couple of hours this morning when they all went on a whale watch. It was so peaceful. Then they had a 'my dress is prettier than your dress' competition. Not that they called it that. All Mellie told her friends was to get soft yellow dresses. They could pick their own so they could wear it after the wedding."

"What a good idea." Bea slipped a stem of lavender into one of the arrangements for the bride's table at the reception.

"You'd think, but we've got everything from a strapless cocktail dress about two sizes too small for the girl wearing it to a granny muumuu thing that completely swallows the skinny chick wearing it. They both look like a wardrobe malfunction waiting to happen." She sighed. "I like the symmetry of all the dresses being alike."

"What did Ryan do during the fashion show?" Kaylee asked.

Lorie winced. "He held up an index finger, tilted his head in the general direction of the door, and disappeared."

"When do his best man and groomsmen arrive?" Bea took two green florist foam spheres and wrapped the rounds with water-resistant florist's tape so they looked like tiny green basketballs.

"There are no men coming."

"None? Then what's he doing for a best man?" Kaylee grabbed the large plastic trash container on wheels and swept the discarded leaves and stems littering the worktable into it.

"I introduced him to Reese a couple of hours ago."

"He's going to have a stranger as his best man?" Kaylee was scandalized. "How sad is that?"

"I know. I'm not sure he has male friends. At least Reese cleans up nicely. He'll look good in the pictures, and you'll be able to see his eyebrows." Lorie slapped her hand over her mouth. "Sorry. There's nothing wrong with Ryan being so fair that his eyebrows blend with his skin. I must work at being nice. The guy's going to be my son-in-law." She dropped her head into her hands in despair. "My son-in-law!"

"I've never seen Reese in anything but jeans and old flannel shirts." Kaylee began arranging the flowers in buckets by color. "It'll be interesting to see him in a suit."

"Not tomorrow. Ryan is just wearing dress pants and a white shirt. Reese assures him he can match that."

"So how many large arrangements at the wedding?" Bea asked.

"Two. I was going to have one behind the officiant, but then I figured he'd block the flowers I'm spending big money on. So one on either side of the arbor."

"Sounds good. Who is doing the ceremony?" Bea asked.

"The mayor." Lorie sighed. "I tried every minister and priest on the island because I think this marriage needs an extra dose of God's blessing to survive, but they're all booked for other weddings and have been for months."

"It's prime season for weddings. Kaylee's got them for the next four weekends."

"I do?" Kaylee began to sweat. "You can't leave me!" Even with online video tutorials, she'd never make it. She should have stayed in Seattle and looked for another teaching job.

Mary walked into the workroom carrying a large box, an online shipping label on the side. "For you, Kaylee."

"What? I didn't order anything."

"Dr. Katherine Bleu. It says so right on the label."

Kaylee took the box, which was relatively light for its size. She checked the label. "This isn't a computer-generated mailing label. It's handwritten."

"Who cares?" Bea waved her hand. "Open it."

Kaylee split the tape with a pair of shears and peeled back the flaps. Pages of *The Orcas Gazette*, the weekly paper, blocked her view of the contents. She peeled back the newssheet and stared. She felt the blood drain from her face.

"What is it?" Lorie tried to see without leaving her stool.

"Kaylee?" Bea's voice was full of concern. "What's wrong?"

"It's a bouquet."

"How lovely," Lorie gushed. "You have an admirer."

Kaylee shook her head. "I don't think so." She reached in, careful to wrap the newspaper around the contents, and lifted out *Aconitum lycoctonum*, *Conium maculatum*, and *Rosa nutkana*.

"Wolfsbane, poison hemlock and dead wild roses." Her insides twisted. "Someone sent me a bouquet of poisonous plants and dead flowers."

# 14

$B$ea reared back as if the sender of the bouquet had struck her, her face ashen. "Get them out of here!"

"Who would be so nasty?" Lorie gaped at the ugly plants.

Kaylee shuddered and turned to Mary. "Where did this come from? Who delivered it?"

Mary's face was crinkled with concern. "A teenage boy brought them. Let me see if I can catch him." She hurried from the room.

As the shock of such a hateful "gift" lessened, Kaylee looked in the box again. "There's a card." She pulled it out and read aloud: "Keep your pretty nose out of things that aren't your business. Or else your little dog . . ."

Kaylee dropped the card as if it burned. "Where's Bear?"

Hearing his name, Bear trotted to her, abandoning the collection of discarded leaves he'd been pushing around with his nose. She grabbed him and held him so tightly he squirmed to get down. As her heartbeat returned to normal, she kissed his forehead and set him on the floor. He went back to chasing leaves.

"What does that mean, keep your nose out?" Bea asked.

"I don't know." But she had an idea.

"Maybe it's from the woman at the university who got your job."

"Somebody got a job that should have been yours?" Lorie frowned. "Then you should be the one sending mean notes, not the other way around."

"I agree. She won. Why would she care about me any longer?"

Kaylee glanced at her grandmother. "And it was never my job."

"It should have been."

Kaylee agreed, though she didn't say so out loud.

Bea took a deep, shaky breath. "Is there anyone else who might be mad at you? Who would do such a hateful thing?"

"You haven't been here on Orcas long enough for someone to be this upset with you," Lorie said.

"You're right. Everyone I've met has been friendly and kind."

But what about people off the island? Jules? She smiled grimly. When someone was as mean and petty as he, he automatically became the first suspect, even if she had no idea how he could have known what she had found.

But given all Jules's legal shenanigans over the past seven years, would Isaac tell him about the book before he knew exactly what he had? She doubted it. And even if Isaac had told him, why would he send her such a threatening bouquet? It wasn't as if doing so would make the pages and drive disappear. Besides he now had two books of his own to enjoy the income from. Why would he get so upset with her?

"I got him!" Mary came panting into the room, pulling a gangly boy of about fifteen behind her. He wore jeans and a faded Seahawks jersey not quite long enough in the arms. He looked like he wanted to be anywhere but here.

"Tell them what you told me," Mary ordered.

"I didn't do anything wrong." He looked like Bear when Kaylee yelled at him for some offense. The only thing missing was the tail between the legs.

"We're not saying you did." Mary patted him on the arm. "We just need to know where the flowers came from."

"Flowers were in the box?" He glanced at it in surprise. "I didn't know they sold flowers online."

"These weren't ordered online. Someone just used a box to make it look like they were. The question is who."

"Well I got the box from some guy."

"We need more." Lorie leaned forward eagerly, and Kaylee bet she was keeping mental notes for one of her books.

The kid looked thoughtful. "He had on a ball cap pulled low and sunglasses, the reflective kind so I was looking at myself when I looked at him. Creepy. He had black hair pulled back in a ponytail. I remember the hair because I like mine long, and my mom is always on my back to get it cut."

"Good," Kaylee encouraged. "Anything else? What was he wearing?"

"Maybe jeans and a windbreaker?" The kid shrugged. "Or maybe I just think that because that's what I usually wear when I take the ferry."

Kaylee sighed. The culprit could be anyone. "How did you come in contact with the guy?"

"I was at the landing when the ferry came in. I go down and hang around, and sometimes they give me work. Sweeping up. Taking out the trash."

"And?" Kaylee prompted.

He cleared his throat. "So cars are pulling off and people who walked on in Anacortes are walking off, some with their bikes, some with backpacks full of stuff, all coming for the weekend. I figure they're going over to Moran State Park, you know."

"I know." Moran was a favorite for lots of outdoorsy people.

"So suddenly this guy is there, right in front of me. 'Take this box to The Flower Patch for me, will you, kid? I'll pay you well. I don't have time because I have to get back on the ferry.' He hands me the box and a fifty dollar bill. I never saw that big a bill before." The kid looked suddenly worried. "I don't have to give it back, do I?"

"Not as far as we're concerned," Kaylee assured him. "You're sure the guy got back on the ferry?"

"He was in line when I left to bring the box here."

"With a car or as a walk-on?"

"A walk-on."

A walk-on who might get off at any of the other stops the ferry made.

"You need to call the sheriff's office, Kaylee," Mary said. "If these flowers aren't a direct death threat, at the very least they're meant to scare and harass."

Kaylee looked at the boy. "What's your name?"

"Bobby Tumbrull." He tipped his head toward the box. "How can flowers be bad?"

Kaylee ignored his question and asked one of her own. "Can you hang around for a bit so you can talk to the sheriff?"

Now that he knew he wasn't in trouble, Bobby was beginning to enjoy himself. "This is so cool. Sure I'll stay."

Ten minutes later Nick Durham walked into The Flower Patch. Fifteen minutes after that, Bobby was sent on his way, clearly eager to tell his friends about his part in the caper. A half hour later, Bea announced she was tired and needed to go home.

Kaylee glanced at her watch. Four o'clock. "Go ahead. We're ready for the signing and we've done all we can do today for the wedding."

Bea stood, holding the table when she wobbled.

"Grandma!" Kaylee was at her side immediately.

Bea patted Kaylee's arm. "Don't fuss, dear. All I need is a nap."

"Let me drive you home."

Bea straightened and started for the door. "I'll let you know if I ever need a taxi driver."

Kaylee bit back her worried comment. "Yes, ma'am."

"That's my girl."

"Drop me at the inn?" Lorie asked.

"Done. Let's go."

As they left, the bell on the front door jingled, indicating a customer.

"I'm on it." Mary left the workroom.

Kaylee sat on one of the stools and Nick leaned against the table, arms crossed, watching her.

"So are you going to tell me?" he asked.

Kaylee swallowed. "Tell you what?"

"I don't know. That's why I asked."

Kaylee decided to ask her own question. "Do you think this—" she flicked a hand at the box still sitting on the worktable, "—has anything to do with the break-in at the Ashfords'?"

Nick raised his eyebrows. "Now why in the world would I think that?"

*Why indeed. If you didn't know I have the "missing" folder, why would you think there was a connection?* A break-in and theft. A nasty floral gift. They were nothing alike. She should have kept her mouth shut.

He waited, and she fought fidgeting. Fidgeting would make her look guilty. An innocent person would sit quietly because she had nothing to hide.

"I didn't break in and take the folder," she blurted. At least the first part was true.

"I never thought you did."

"Good."

"But I think you know more about it than you're saying."

She dropped her gaze. She'd never been a good liar. It took too much energy to remember what you had said. If you told the truth, you only had to remember one thing. Trouble was, she couldn't tell the whole truth yet.

"Who have you upset recently?"

She looked at the box as if Cleopatra's asp was going to slither out and bite her. "I don't know." It came out as a whisper, so she cleared her throat and tried again. "I don't know."

"All three of the flowers grow wild in the San Juans as well as the Pacific Northwest in general."

"So anyone would have access. Ironically there's a poison hemlock plant growing in the Ashfords' front yard. You should check to see if it's still there."

He shrugged that suggestion away. "Of course the newspaper pins the geography to the San Juans."

Kaylee rubbed her arms to ease the chill. "Yes."

"I wish you'd tell me what you're afraid to tell me."

She felt her face flush.

He straightened. "But I can't make you. The days of rubber truncheons and bright lights are gone. These days you have to choose to cooperate."

She wanted to. She really did.

"Do you think your life is in danger?"

She stared at him. He was serious. "No! Poisonous flowers are nasty, but they're a long way from actually harming me."

He nodded and suddenly smiled. "I can't wait until these cases are over."

"Me neither!"

"Probably for different reasons. I want to ask you out, but I can't while I'm working with you on a professional basis." With another of those winks, he strolled from the workroom, the box of flowers under his arm.

Kaylee stared after him. *He wants to ask me out?* She couldn't help but smile. When was the last time she'd actually gone on a date? All the men she knew at the university were married. She'd always told herself she didn't mind her solitary Friday and

Saturday nights, but it would be fun to spend a weekend night with someone besides Bear. Maybe he'd take her to The Ideal Meal, and she could see why everyone liked it.

She was sweeping the workroom floor when Nick appeared in the doorway.

"Hi." She smiled at him. "I thought you left."

"You need to come with me. Your grandmother needs you."

Kaylee went cold all over. "What happened?"

"Sorry. I didn't mean to scare you. She's fine physically. She just had the shock of coming home to a house that's been burglarized."

"What?" She grabbed her purse and laptop and ran, pausing only long enough to collect Bear from his nap in the ray of sunshine that fell through the front windows. Nick was already jogging toward his cruiser as Kaylee looked helplessly at Mary.

"Go!" Mary made shooing motions. "I'll lock up when it's time."

"Thanks. My hands are shaking so badly I'd never get the key in the lock."

As she hurried to her car, she held Bear close. He felt her agitation and gave her a lick on the cheek.

"That's my boy." She put him on the passenger seat and raced around the car to her side. Kaylee flew down the road, taking the two and a half miles to Wildflower Cottage in record time.

"Grandma!" She raced for the steps only to hear shrill barking behind her. She did a quick backpedal.

"Sorry, Bear." She opened the car door, and the relieved Bear jumped out. She left him to take care of business and sprinted into the house.

She found Bea and Nick standing in the door to her bedroom, the room that had been Ed's office. She peered over their shoulders and felt her stomach turn over.

The room was total chaos. Everything she'd already unpacked was pulled from drawers, and what she hadn't yet unpacked was pulled from the boxes and suitcases. The mattress was pushed off the bed, and the bedding lay in a tangle on the floor. The desk had been rifled, and the contents were strewn on the floor. But most distressing was the state of Ed's journals. They were dumped in a pile, pages ripped out, torn like confetti, and scattered around the room.

She stood in the doorway, swallowing convulsively and trying not to throw up. "Who? Why?"

Bea stepped behind her and held her close, resting her head against Kaylee's back. Kaylee turned and wrapped her arms around Bea. She could feel her grandmother shaking. How must she feel seeing not only her home torn up, but the journals desecrated as well?

Nick took charge. "Why don't you two go into the living room, and let me take a good look around here. Make yourselves a cup of tea or something."

Kaylee nodded blankly.

"Then I'm going to ask you if you see anything missing."

Kaylee looked at him in disbelief. "How am I supposed to tell if anything's gone with this mess?"

"I know. But you can check for missing electronics—laptop, tablet, phone. How about cash? Drugs? Most home invasions are for easily portable items that have a quick and ready market."

"Drugs?" Bea drew herself up to her full height and turned an appalled and outraged gaze on Nick. "No one in this house uses drugs." She seemed to reconsider. "At least the kind you're talking about. I've got a medicine chest full of stuff in my bathroom."

"It's okay, Grandma. He has to ask." Kaylee forced herself to concentrate. "I had my laptop and phone with me at the store.

I left my tablet in the living room this morning. I was checking images of bridal bouquets before I went to work. It should be on the credenza by the TV."

Nick walked through the house and came back with Kaylee's tablet in hand.

She took it from him, remembering when creating a beautiful flower arrangement was her biggest concern. "Is the living room a shambles too?"

"No, but the back sliding door is open. I'm assuming it was closed when you left for work this morning?" He looked from Kaylee to Bea.

"It was," Kaylee said. "I was here at the house cutting flowers in the meadow about eleven or eleven thirty. I came in the house to get bug spray and the kitchen to get bottled water. Everything was fine at that time, and I locked up as usual when I left. Then I went to the Ashford place to cut flowers there."

"So this happened somewhere between noon and now."

"The guy with the ponytail?" Kaylee suggested. "Maybe he never got on the ferry."

"Maybe." Nick looked at Bea. "What time do you usually come home from work?"

"At the end of the workday, some time after five."

"But you came home at least an hour early today."

"You think I scared off whoever it was?"

"The open slider suggests that."

Bea shuddered and Kaylee's heart broke at how frail her grandmother looked. She was usually so full of energy and curiosity it was easy to forget her age.

"Come on, Grandma. Let's go sit in the living room while Nick looks around. In fact I could use a cup of tea."

"Yes." Bea walked to the living room and sank into her favorite chair. She closed her eyes and rested her head against the chair back. "Never in all the years I've lived here has something like this happened."

Kaylee knelt in front of her grandmother and took her hands. "It's okay, Grandma."

Bea made a dissenting noise.

"You're right." Kaylee squeezed her grandmother's cold hands. "It isn't okay. But we're okay."

A knock on the front door sounded. "Bea? Kaylee? Are you all right? What's happened?"

Kaylee turned and saw Mary in the doorway with a man Kaylee assumed was her husband, the former mail carrier.

Mary homed in on Bea, and her voice cracked when she spoke. "I was so afraid something happened to you. When Nick came running back into the shop, and he and Kaylee went running out, and Kaylee drove off without even buckling Bear in, I was so afraid."

"I'm fine," Bea held out a hand to Mary. "A bit shaken up, but not hurt at all."

"Bear!" Kaylee jumped to her feet. "I left him outside."

"Are you talking about this guy?" Mary's husband stepped clear of the doorjamb, and there was Bear, tucked comfortably in his arm. He grinned at Kaylee. "By the way, I'm Mary's husband, Herb."

Herb set the dog on the floor, and Bear raced to Kaylee. She grabbed him and held him close while he covered her face with kisses.

"So what happened?" Mary took a seat on the arm of Bea's chair, holding her hand.

Bea's eyes filled with tears. "Someone broke in. He—" Her voice caught. "He trashed Ed's office. His journals!"

Herb frowned as he took a seat on the couch. "Why would anyone care about Ed's journals?"

Mary sat up straight. "Those pages you showed us."

"Thankfully the police have that journal." Kaylee set Bear on the floor, and he careened happily from person to person for their adoration and scratches.

"What's going on here?" Mary sounded as if she took all the troubles personally. "First the flowers and now this."

"Don't forget the Ashfords' home was burglarized too." Kaylee sank to the floor at Bea's feet, resting her head against her grandmother's knee. Bear climbed into her lap.

"I heard about that break-in," said a new voice. "It's all over town."

DeeDee Wilcox walked in with Jessica and Luke Roberts right behind her. "Mary called and told us something was wrong here, so we've come," DeeDee said. "Andy would be here too, but he's home with our daughters. We were afraid to bring them when we didn't know what the trouble was." She walked directly to Bea. "You're okay?"

A touch of Bea's spunk reappeared as she gave all the Petal Pushers a disbelieving look. "You all expected to find me dead, didn't you? Come on. Admit it."

"Well, you know how Oliver's leaves have been drooping," Jessica said by way of explanation while her husband rolled his eyes behind her.

"The geranium that predicts calamity?" Kaylee had to laugh. "He's been right on point. You've just been worried about the wrong catastrophe."

"What's a police car doing here?" Lorie Loblinski stood in the doorway looking worried. "Bea, are you okay?"

"What is it with you people?" Bea demanded. "Just because I'm old doesn't mean I'm getting ready to kick the bucket."

"They love you, Grandma," Kaylee whispered. "Thank them for caring."

Instead, Bea glared at them all. They all smiled back.

"Is everything all right?" another voice, this one male, called from over Lorie's shoulder. "Nick's cruiser is here and all these other cars. Is Bea all right?"

Reese stepped into the room, and Kaylee blinked. He had on dress pants and a dress shirt and tie. In place of his work boots he wore carefully shined dress shoes. Lorie was more than right when she'd said he cleaned up well.

Kaylee looked from Reese to Lorie. "I thought you two were at the rehearsal dinner."

"On my way," Lorie said.

"Me too." Reese smiled at Bea. "I'm glad to see you're fine. I was worried there for a minute."

"Yeah, me too." Lorie put her hands on her hips. "So what did happen here? I'll never enjoy my dinner if I don't know. Of course I won't enjoy my dinner anyway." Her expression morphed from curious about Bea's problem to disgust. "I saw them kissing!"

"I assume you mean Melanie and Ryan?" Bea asked.

"Most about-to-be-married couples kiss." Jessica was trying not to laugh. "You'd better prepare yourself, Lorie. They'll kiss again at the end of the ceremony."

Lorie shuddered. "I'm fine with people kissing. I write about people kissing. It's just—"

Her expression changed again to deep regret and sorrow. "I'd hoped for so much more for her."

In the silence that followed, Reese put an arm around Lorie's shoulders and squeezed. She rested her head on his shoulder, not as a drama queen enjoying a man's attention as much as a woman with a broken heart being comforted.

Nick walked into the silence and halted abruptly when he saw all the people. "Whoa! Where did you all come from?"

"They all thought I'd died." Bea sat up straight and proud. "I fooled them."

Nick grinned at her. "You sure did." He turned to Kaylee and his smile fell away. He gestured toward the ruined bedroom. "Kaylee, can we talk?"

# 15

Feeling she was headed to the guillotine, Kaylee put Bear on the floor. He promptly ran to Reese who crouched to give him a good tummy rub.

Nick stepped into the bedroom and motioned her in. He shut the door. "Too many interested ears."

As she looked around the room, Kaylee felt again the deep sense of violation. Someone had handled her things without permission, damaging many of them, showing no regard for personal possessions or privacy. How long would it be before she felt safe here again?

And that thought made her angry at whoever had done this to her grandmother and her. What right did this person have to take away the joy in their home, the feeling of being secure inside their cottage? The anger was a shot of steel that stiffened her spine.

Nick eyed her. "Whenever a crime happens, one of the first things an officer of the law asks is who benefits from it? I ask myself that question here, and I don't know the answer. Do you?"

"No, I don't."

If his expression was any indication, he didn't believe her, but it was the truth. She had no idea who the bad guy was. Why he'd been here, yes, she had a strong suspicion. But who? No idea at all.

She placed her hands on her hips and looked Nick in the eye, trying to look honest and believable. Then she thought that position probably looked too confrontational, so she let her arms fall to her sides. But seeing again all the chaos in the room made her cold through and through. She folded her arms across her chest to try and get warm.

"Two break-ins in one day." Nick shook his head. "Back in LA where I used to work, stuff like this wasn't unusual. Here, it's very unusual. Then there are the nasty flowers sent to a pretty lady. Add an old journal with suggestions of murder and the mysterious disappearance of the writer of that journal—who just happens to be the grandfather of the flower recipient and vandalism victim."

Kaylee stared at him mutely. What could she say?

"What do these things have in common, Kaylee?" He didn't wait for an answer. "You. You are the connector of the seemingly unrelated dots, the little black line that runs from event to event."

She hugged herself tighter.

"What's the picture you're drawing, Kaylee? Do you even know?" He studied her, brows furrowed, eyes intent. "Talk to me."

She threw her arms wide. "How could what happened to my grandfather five years ago have anything to do with the ugly flowers or this break-in?"

"I don't know. That's why I'm asking you."

Kaylee grabbed a sweater lying in a pile of things pulled from one of her suitcases. She thrust her arms in the sleeves and wrapped it close, hoping it would ease the chill. It didn't.

What could she say without breaking her word? "Call Isaac Ashford. He can tell you what you need to know. Some of it anyway." He probably had no more idea than she who the culprit was.

Nick looked surprised. "Porter Ashford's son?"

"His oldest. A very nice man." And he could release her from her promise and give her permission to hand the folder and drive to Nick.

"I assume you have contact information?"

She pulled out her phone and read off Isaac's number. Rather than write it down, Nick studied her.

She couldn't meet his gaze and stared at the pull in the sleeve of her sweater, a pull that hadn't been there before the vandal's manhandling. His eyes narrowed. He didn't write the information down. "You already spoke with Isaac, didn't you? About the robbery at his parents' house." And Isaac hadn't mentioned the book or papers because if he had, Nick wouldn't be asking her.

"I find it interesting that you have his number nice and handy on your phone. Probably from your call log, since you didn't seem to be scrolling through contacts looking for him. I take that to mean you've spoken with him recently."

She started picking at the pull in her sweater.

"Go back to the living room, Kaylee." His voice sounded tired and disappointed. With her. There was no wink, no mild flirtation like before.

She grabbed the doorknob, happy to leave the room and the inquisition and hopefully the guilt.

"And Kaylee." He met her eyes squarely when she looked back at him. "Be careful. I don't know who is behind all of this, but someone is not at all happy with you."

Kaylee closed the door behind her. She paused in the hall and leaned against the wall, eyes shut. How had she gotten in such an uncomfortable and dangerous situation? The answer to that question was obvious. She'd taken the folder. A better question was why was she in danger? And from whom? With a deep sigh, she pushed off the wall and went to check on her grandmother.

When she walked into the main part of the house, she found a completely different scene than she had left. Lorie and Reese were gone, presumably to the rehearsal dinner, but everyone else was still there. The women were in the kitchen and the men were in the living room watching a sports program, Bear lying at their feet.

She wandered into the kitchen where Mary and Jessica were busy cutting veggies for a salad. DeeDee hung up her phone. "Andy will be here in about fifteen or twenty minutes with pizza and the girls." She glanced at Kaylee. "I ordered a plain one, one with sausage and mushrooms, and one with everything but anchovies. I hope you like one of them."

"I do. All of them."

"Good." DeeDee took her place at the table with the veggies. "Whoever ends up cutting the onion, would you put it in a separate dish? The girls draw the line at onions, especially Polly, and I want them to eat some salad."

"What shall I do?" Kaylee asked, overwhelmed with all the energy pulsing in the air.

Jessica looked up from gutting a yellow pepper. "Don't worry about anything, Kaylee. Have some hot tea with your grandmother."

Bea held out her hand. "Sit with me, sweetheart. I think we've both earned the right to be waited on tonight."

Kaylee collapsed into a chair, and almost by magic a pot of tea appeared at her elbow.

"Peppermint," Jessica said. "Very soothing."

Kaylee inhaled the aroma and felt some of the tension in her shoulders relax. Jessica set a china cup covered in pansies in front of her and filled it from the pot. Kaylee added two sugars and took a sip. "Wonderful."

Bear appeared, drawn by her voice, and put his front paws on her knee. She picked him up and gave him a kiss on the top of his head. With a happy sigh, he settled in her lap.

"Do you need anything more for tomorrow, DeeDee?" Mary tore the last of the lettuce. "What can we do for the signing tomorrow?"

"I think things are in order." DeeDee slid the thin slices of cucumber into the salad bowl and picked up a Vidalia onion. "I'll go in early tomorrow morning for last-minute preparations."

"What time?" Lettuce done, Mary began working on baby carrots. "I'll come as early as you want."

"Kaylee will get the flowers out of the cooler and bring them over," Bea said. "We made little corsages and boutonnieres for everyone."

DeeDee grinned with pleasure. "How lovely. My main worry is that Ward Meacham won't make the early ferry."

"Not a problem," Bea said absently as she concentrated on pouring more tea into her cup, which was covered with daffodils. "He's already here."

"What?" DeeDee, Jessica, and Mary spoke in chorus.

"Grandma!"

Bea slapped a hand over her mouth. "Forget I said that."

"Too late." DeeDee stood in front of her with her hands on her hips. "Talk."

Bea looked at Kaylee, eyes wide.

Kaylee had to laugh at her grandmother's expression. "I don't think it matters anymore, Grandma." She looked at DeeDee. "He's been staying at Mermaid Cottage, taking a couple of days' break from his tour."

"He used to rent Mermaid Cottage for the summer back before he became famous," Bea said. "It was a pretty awful place back then, but it had a great location in a little cove."

DeeDee wasn't interested in the cottage. She made little fist pumps. "I'm so glad to know he's here. Now I can sleep tonight without worrying that my big celebrity might not make it."

The whole time they prepared dinner, the Petals talked. Kaylee sat and watched, amazed and fascinated at their ease and lack of competition. Social gatherings at the university had felt like a constant jockeying for position, and she'd been as guilty as the others. Here there were just friends who liked each other, supported each other, and often finished each other's sentences.

"I've got mini chocolate cream puffs and tiny chocolate tarts for tomorrow," Jessica said. "Mary, can you help me carry all the beverages and stuff to Dee's?"

"Sounds good. It'll give me a chance to sneak a cream—"

"No sneaking allowed!" Jessica's expression was severe. "I set aside half a dozen for you and Luke, and you can have them after the signing."

Mary's grin was euphoric.

"What about me?" DeeDee demanded.

"A full dozen."

"Twice as many?" Mary pretended to be hurt.

"She has twice as many people, and she's been running this whole thing."

"What about us?" Bea indicated Kaylee and herself.

"Got half a dozen for you too."

DeeDee looked at Kaylee with a straight face. "It's called buying friends. Works every time."

"The Queen of Chocolate takes a bow." Jessica bent at the waist with great flourish.

"Bea." DeeDee grew serious. "Don't push yourself tomorrow. Come to the signing only if you want to. You and Kaylee have had a rough day."

Bea looked at the refrigerator humming in the corner. "Didn't you see the cheese in there? We have to use it or we'll be eating cheese forever!"

"We'll get it all ready tonight," Mary promised. "Then all Kaylee has to do is bring it to the store."

By the time DeeDee's husband, Andy, arrived with their girls and the pizza, the dining room table had been extended, chairs had been found, and a huge salad and four bottles of dressing awaited. Beverages were handed out and everyone grabbed silverware and napkins.

Just before they all sat, DeeDee ushered the two girls forward. "Kaylee, I'd like you to meet my girls. This is Zoe." A cute, blue-eyed girl smiled, her brown hair stuffed into a messy ponytail. "And this is Polly." A cherubic, blond pixie grinned, a half-grown eyetooth adding to the adorable quotient.

"I'm delighted to meet you." Kaylee smiled back.

"I'm eight," Polly announced. "And she's eleven." She jerked a thumb at her sister. "I'm gonna be in third grade and she's in sixth. I do gymnastics and she plays baseball. Not girls' softball. Little League with the boys. I can do cartwheels and backflips. Want to see?" Her brown eyes were eager.

"Uh." Kaylee glanced around quickly, not certain where there was room for any of Polly's promised maneuvers given all the people milling around.

"Not now, sweetie." DeeDee turned her daughter toward the table. "Time to eat."

Nick appeared in the room, and Kaylee walked to him. "Want some pizza? You're welcome to stay."

"Thanks, but no. I need to go write a report." He handed her a card. "My contact information. If you suddenly feel the urge to talk, call anytime. I mean that anytime part." He fixed her with a steely look.

She swallowed. "Okay." She missed that wink.

"I know you've testified for the police before back in Seattle. I know your testimony has helped convict criminals, including a murderer. I don't get this reluctance, Kaylee. I don't like it."

"Thanks for all you've done, Nick."

"Nick," Mary called. "Can we start cleaning up in there? We'd like to put it back in order for Bea and Kaylee."

"Go ahead. I've documented everything with pictures and video and checked for any evidence."

"Thanks." Mary gave a little wave.

Nick let himself out. Kaylee sighed. He was not a happy camper.

In spite of the heaviness of her heart, Kaylee found herself enjoying her new friends. She knew she liked Mary, Jessica, and DeeDee, but she decided she liked their husbands too. They were good men, funny and kind. They treated Zoe and Polly with respect, and in turn the girls were well-behaved. Mary dished up the salad, and the pizza disappeared in short order. The last glasses were being loaded into the dishwasher when Reese reappeared.

"Good timing," Mary called. "You're just in time for an ice cream cone."

Reese held up a hand. "Nothing for me, thanks. That rehearsal dinner was wonderful, and I ate everything on my plate."

"I didn't know you knew the groom," Jessica said. "How'd you manage to meet him when Lorie never had?"

"Never met him before yesterday." Reese shrugged. "We handymen come in handy in many ways, though being a best man is a new one for me."

"Okay, everyone." Mary clapped for attention. "It's time to tackle the bedroom. DeeDee, you remake the bed. Polly and Zoe, you can take the dirty sheets to the laundry area."

"We can start the machine," Polly piped up. "We do our laundry sometimes to help Mom."

"That's so sweet," Kaylee said as the girls skipped out of the room.

DeeDee and Andy chuckled. Seeing Kaylee's confused look, DeeDee said, "They are very helpful by nature."

"But sometimes Polly gets a little . . . overzealous with the detergent," Andy added. "We usually have to rewash whatever she 'launders' for us."

"I'll get the clothes on the floor," Jessica said, pulling their attention back to business. "I'll fold them and pile them on the bed when DeeDee has made it." She glanced at Kaylee. "Or do you want me to wash them all?"

"For now, just pick them up," Kaylee said. "I'll take care of the washing after the wedding."

"I'll take the desk," Mary said.

"What about me?" Bea asked.

"See that chair over there?" Mary jerked her head at Bea's favorite chair in the living room. "Sit there and watch TV. The guys'll watch it with you until we need them."

Bea started to protest, but after a slight pause, she nodded. As Kaylee watched her grandmother take her seat, she realized anew how much the chaos of the day had taken out of her.

As the Petals headed off to cleanup detail, Lorie walked in. She looked pale and uncertain, very un-Lorie-like, to say nothing of very, very un-Lorelei-like. She saw Kaylee and headed for her, stumbling over nothing as she came.

# 16

Kaylee rushed to her. "Lorie! Are you all right?"

"I don't know." She seemed lost.

"Here, have a seat at the kitchen table." She took Lorie's elbow and guided her to a chair. "Is it Melanie? Has she done something more to upset you?"

Lorie sat heavily and dropped her head to her hands. "You could say so."

*Peppermint tea*, Kaylee thought. It had helped her. She quickly microwaved a mug of it. "Here, Lorie. Drink."

Lorie took the mug and held it between her hands. "He's here, Kaylee."

Lorie seemed to think that explained everything, but it didn't. "Who's here?" Kaylee asked.

"I didn't expect him. I didn't know Mellie had asked him, though why wouldn't she?" Lorie set down the mug so as not to splash herself with the steaming tea. She held out a shaking hand. "Look! I'm a wreck. Isn't it ridiculous? You'd think after three years I'd be over him."

"I take it you're not talking about Ryan."

"Ryan the Loser? Are you kidding? He makes me sick, but he doesn't make me a nervous wreck."

"Then who?"

"Dennis. My Dennis." Her lips started to quiver, and she pressed a hand to them. "Oh, Kaylee, I don't know what to do or how to act."

"Dennis, your ex-husband?" Kaylee wanted to be clear on this important point.

Lorie stood and began pacing. "He's not really my ex. We never got around to making the divorce official. But he left three years ago. He came walking into the rehearsal dinner tonight as big as you please, smiling at everyone, shaking hands, kissing all the ladies. Even me." Her hand went to her cheek, and Kaylee guessed that to be the site of his kiss.

"He just said, 'Hello, Lorie,' in that deep mellow voice I always loved. I thought I'd faint. I really did. Just like some pampered beauty in one of my historical romances, but she'd have the excuse of a corset."

"And you didn't wear yours tonight."

"Cute." She fell back in her seat. "Mellie should have told me. Then I'd have been prepared."

"Then you'd have worried and worried, and it would have changed nothing."

Lorie sighed deeply. "You're probably right. I know I won't sleep tonight worrying about seeing him again tomorrow. I'll have circles under my eyes for the signing. Fans are coming from all over, and I'm very pleased. But I'll look like a troll."

"Hardly a troll, Lorie, and that's what concealer's for."

Lorie was too busy being dramatic for that practical tip to stop her rant. "And there's the wedding, where they'll take pictures. Pictures! My black circles will be preserved for posterity!"

Kaylee sighed mentally. Girl confessions weren't her strong suit, especially ones laced with histrionics, but faced with Lorie's distress, she had to try. "Are you mad at Melanie for asking him? Are you mad at Dennis for coming to give away his daughter? Are you just mad at Dennis? Sad? Confused? Was he a problem at the dinner?" Kaylee imagined him blustering around, putting everyone on edge with bad behavior.

"Dennis, a problem?" Lorie looked shocked at the suggestion. "Never. He's always been Mr. Smooth. He has all the style and class I don't. I'm loud and pushy, especially when I play Lorelei, but he's always just right."

A dreamy look washed over her face. "And handsome. So handsome. He doesn't look a day older, still slim and hardly any gray. Just that gentleman's gray at the temples."

"So you're happy to see him?"

The dreamy expression disappeared, and Lorie looked like the sad and disappointed older woman she was. "It hurts to see him because I still love him. I do. I miss him." The last came out in a whisper.

So Lorie loved Dennis, but they were separated. "Did he take up with someone else? Is that what broke you up?" Kaylee had a terrible thought. *Maybe he brought a new woman along.* Not Mr. Smooth if so.

"Dennis? Unfaithful? Never. He's Mr. True Blue."

Then what? "Did you take up with someone?"

"Me?" She looked horrified. "Never. There's no man alive who could take his place."

"Then I'm confused. What happened?"

"I don't know!" It was a wail.

"Your marriage fell apart and you don't know why?"

"I don't know why. Isn't that pathetic? All I know is I came home from Writers Coterie three years ago, and Dennis was leaving. 'What's wrong?' I asked. 'Don't leave me,' I begged. 'I know how you really feel,' he said. 'I understand. I won't stand in your way.' 'How I really feel about what?' I asked. 'Don't be such a gentleman. Stand in my way. Please!' But he was gone."

"Lorie, I'm so sorry."

"Yeah, me too. We were like a happily-ever-after couple I wrote in one of my books, but we were *real*."

"Hey! Look at me," a little voice sang. "I'm a bride!" Polly walked into the kitchen with the elasticized corner of Kaylee's bottom bedsheet on her head like a flapper's headband, the rest of the sheet fanning out behind her like a train. "I'm on my way to marry a very rich man."

Even Lorie in her heartbreak couldn't help smiling at the adorable little girl. "Sounds like a good idea to me."

"That's what my dad says. He wants to retire and live off his new son." She held out her hands. "I need a bouquet. You got any flowers?"

"I have a store full of them," Kaylee said, "but I don't have any here."

"Can you go get some for me?"

"I'm sorry. I can't. They're for a real wedding tomorrow."

"A real wedding?" Polly's eyes lit up. "Can I come to the real wedding? I only ever saw them on TV."

"I'll tell your mom you're invited," Lorie said with a smile.

"When? I can get her right now."

Lorie held up a hand. "Don't bother her now. She's busy. I'll talk to her tomorrow. I'm going to be in her store signing books."

"You're one of the writers?"

"I am."

Polly squealed and bolted for the bedroom, her forgotten and abandoned bridal veil falling to the floor. "Hey, Mom, one of the writers is having a real wedding tomorrow, and she said I can come. Can I? I never went to a real wedding before."

Zoe appeared and began gathering up the veil. She looked shyly at Lorie. "Can we really come?"

"If your mom can bring you."

"Where is it?"

"Right here in the backyard."

"Right here is good. Thank you." Zoe smiled her quiet but charming smile. "It's good if we come because Polly says she's going to design wedding dresses when she grows up, but only after she wins her gold medal at the Olympics."

"Good for her. A woman should have goals. How about you?"

"I'm going to be a scientist." Zoe did a little foot shuffle at the very idea. "I don't know what kind yet, but I *love* science."

"Be a plant taxonomist," Kaylee suggested. "It's a good field."

"What is it?" Zoe asked.

"It's what I used to be."

Zoe appeared to be digesting that. "I'll look it up online and see if it sounds interesting. I do like plants." With that she took the discarded sheet off the washing machine.

Kaylee watched her disappear and was relieved to see Lorie smiling after her. "Makes me think of a young Mellie," Lorie said wistfully. She turned to Kaylee, sighed and stood. "I'd better be going. Thanks for listening."

"Wish there was something I could do to help." A demanding daughter, an unimpressive son-in-law-to-be, and an estranged but much-loved husband. Lorie was having a rough time for sure.

"Yeah. I'd rather be dealing with your bad guy any day."

On that happy note, Lorie left.

Reese appeared at Kaylee's elbow. "I wanted to tell you I bought some flowers for the Ashford place. The nursery up the road was having a sale, and I bought a bunch of red, pink, and white flowers. The nursery guy said they'd do well in the shade and bloom until frost. I hope you don't mind."

"Sounds like *Impatiens walleriana*. A very good choice for all that shade."

"I tucked them under the bushes. They're still in their flats. Can I leave their care to you?"

"You can. So how did the rehearsal go?"

"Lorie's husband was there. I thought she'd pass out when

she saw him. I guess no one told her he was coming to give the bride away."

"She was just telling me about it. I feel so bad for her. Tomorrow's going to be a tough day."

"Hey, look what I got." Polly came skipping up. She held out a plastic bag full of confetti. Kaylee recognized the torn pages of Ed's journals, and it gave her heart a twinge. "I picked them up off the floor, and I'm going to use them for the wedding. I can throw them at the bride and groom. Miss Bea said."

"Miss Bea said?" Kaylee looked in the living room and noticed for the first time that her grandmother wasn't in her chair. The woman just had to be where the action was. And if she had said Polly could have the "confetti" from Ed's journals, who was Kaylee to say no? Peering into the bag, Kaylee realized that it wasn't like they would be able to reassemble the pages anyway. The pieces were too small.

"Yep. She said I could tear up more paper at home and make lots and lots of confetti. I could share some with Zoe." Polly studied the fragments in her bag. "I think I'll find colored paper to tear up. That'd make it prettier."

"Be careful with colored paper. It could bleed on the bride's beautiful white dress."

Polly laughed. "Paper doesn't bleed. People bleed." She held out her arm, showing a bandage on her elbow. "See? I bled."

"Polly!" DeeDee's voice echoed down the hall. "More confetti. Come and get it."

"Yay!" And she was off.

It was after eleven before everyone left. Silence descended

on Wildflower Cottage and Kaylee stood in the doorway to her room, Bea beside her.

"It's amazing. It's neater than it was before the break-in. They even emptied my unpacked boxes."

"I saw Luke Roberts carrying the empty ones out to their car to get rid of them for you," Bea told her.

"What about my suitcases?"

"Try the closet."

Kaylee did and found her luggage tucked behind clothes which had been hung neatly on their hangers. "Are you sure you want to leave a place where you have such wonderful friends, Grandma?"

"I wouldn't leave for anyone other than my Lucille. She and I need each other. Sisters to the end. She lives in a retirement community that has various levels of health care and provides for you until you die."

"You're not going to die!"

"If today didn't kill me, I guess I'm not going to for the next little while anyway."

Kaylee looked at the strip of empty shelving in the bookcase. "Grandpa's journals aren't here anymore."

"Andy packed what's left of them in one of your boxes for me. I'm taking them to Arizona. Even if I never read them because they make me too sad, it'll be a piece of Ed by my side."

Kaylee wrapped an arm around her much shorter grandmother and kissed the top of her head. "You made Polly very happy with the 'confetti.'"

"That was DeeDee's idea. The kid thought she was getting a gift, and in reality she was cleaning up the floor. And it's not like I was going to sit around and put the scraps together like a puzzle."

Kaylee opened the second drawer of the dresser where she usually kept her pajamas. Neatly folded sweaters filled the space. She opened two more drawers before she found what she was looking for. She pulled out a sleep shirt with the university logo on it.

"You won't have any trouble sleeping in here tonight, will you?" Bea's brow wrinkled with concern.

"I don't think so. If the room was still in shambles, I probably would, but it's so neat now, I should be fine."

"Good. Then I'm going to bed." Bea reached up and kissed Kaylee's cheek. "Love you, sweetheart."

"Love you back, Grandma."

Kaylee changed quickly, then washed her face and brushed her teeth in the bathroom just across the hall. She grabbed her laptop and climbed into bed.

In spite of all the upset and tension of the day, she'd been looking forward to this time with keen anticipation. She opened Version 5 and jumped back into Riley's life. When she glanced at her watch, she was amazed to see two hours had passed. Much as she hated to stop reading, her eyelids were shutting of their own accord.

She closed the laptop, flipped off the light, and slid down to snuggle into her pillow. Bear awoke in his spot at the foot of the bed and got sleepily to his feet.

Kaylee held out her arms. "Come here."

He made his way to her and settled against her side. She ran her hand over his head, marveling at how comforting his presence was. With a deep sigh, he fell back to sleep.

Kaylee's next conscious thought was that she had to change the tune her phone alarm played. It was too cheery by far to wake up to.

When Kaylee emerged from her bedroom in jeans and her favorite boots and tunic top the next morning, she found Bea at the kitchen table eating toast, orange juice, and a soft-boiled egg.

Bea raised her glass to Kaylee. "You look very pretty this morning."

"Thank you." Not that she was dressed to impress or anything, but all kinds of interesting people would be at the book signing. She carried an old shirt and sneakers to change into for when she started building wedding arrangements.

Bea indicated the toaster. "Ready for you. Just push the slide down."

"Not this morning. I'm going in early. I'll get a cup of coffee from Jess's." She grabbed her keys and jacket. "Come on, Bear. Time to go."

He looked up from his partially eaten breakfast, sniffed, and went back to eating.

Kaylee laughed. "I guess I have time for coffee after all." She poured herself a mugful.

"Here. Take this toast. I'll make more." Bea handed her plate to Kaylee, who slid the toast onto a paper towel. She headed for the front door. "I'm going, Bear."

He took a final chomp of his kibble and ran after her.

Bea, still in her pajamas and robe, followed her. "I'll come later and bring the cheese and stuff. After I get my autographs, I'll cover for you at The Flower Patch so you can go get yours. Then it's bouquets, bouquets, bouquets."

Balancing her toast on top of her mug, Kaylee helped Bear into the car. She climbed in and put her breakfast on the console. Bear eyed the toast with interest.

"Don't even think about it," she said as she buckled him into his harness. Driving to work chomping on cold toast, she noted the fog was burning off the meadows, and the sun showed every sign of shining strong all day. Good news for the wedding. Even good news for the signing. Who wanted to slog through the rain to get a signature?

As she pulled up to The Flower Patch, she noticed a larger-than-usual number of people wandering around Turtle Cove. Several waited outside Death by Chocolate for a table to become available. Kaylee could see Luke Roberts, pressed into service for the busy day, serving a trio of ladies at the four-top in the window. She waved at him, gestured to his apron, and gave a thumbs-up. He gave a slight curtsy, using the apron as his "skirt."

Laughing, she had to admit that Jessica's prediction of a green, crinkly windfall courtesy of Ward Meacham was proving true.

She let herself and Bear into The Flower Patch and headed for the office. She took a deep breath. Even with the flowers tucked away in the refrigeration units for the night, the place had a fragrance that never failed to delight her.

Bear rushed up the stairs ahead of her, ears flapping and tail wagging. He had settled into this new life with his characteristic *joie de vivre*. Just as she thought that, he stopped, gave a bark, and growled deep in his throat.

"Bear?" Kaylee froze and goosebumps rose on her arms. Her dog never growled. She pulled out her phone and hit Nick's number. "Hello? Is anyone here?" she called as she waited for him to pick up.

Like someone would answer if he was still in the shop.

"Just so you know, I'm dialing the police."

Slowly Bear continued toward the office, stopping in the doorway and peering in the room. His tail, which had been stiff as a pike, began to wag, and he disappeared inside.

"Bear, come back here!"

He gave a little come-join-me yip. Determined not to be outdone by a small brown dog's courage, Kaylee walked to the office door. She gasped as she saw Bear standing by an open file cabinet, every drawer pulled out and its contents strewn across the floor.

# 17

Nick took one look at the upended office and said, "We've got to stop meeting like this."

Kaylee scowled. "I'm glad you can joke about it."

"Sorry. It's how I deal with being totally stumped."

Bear stood at Nick's feet, ears perked, tail wagging, tongue lolling. If Nick ever paid him any attention, he was ready to roll over for a good tummy rub. Nick stared Kaylee down with his steely cop eyes, and she felt like rolling over too, not for a tummy rub but with a confession. The compulsion to talk was nearly overwhelming.

The bell on the front door jangled, saving her from owning up to everything she'd ever done wrong in her entire life, including the time she was five and took a candy bar from the grocery store when her mother wasn't looking. When she got home, she was so afraid her mother would walk in while she ate it that she never even unwrapped it. She snuck it to school and left it on her teacher's desk when no one was looking. She'd confessed to her mother three weeks later.

"Customer," she said quietly. No confessions today after all.

"Go." He looked resigned. "I'll be here for a while."

She went and sold two bars of DeeDee's lavender soap and a silk flower arrangement. She was ringing up the sale when Mary came in.

"Just getting the flowers for DeeDee."

"Thanks, Mary."

When Mary came out of the back room with a box of flowers, the customer was gone. "What's Nick doing here?" she asked. "Not another break-in, is it?"

"The office got it this time."

"What in the world is this guy looking for?"

"Whatever it is, he isn't finding it, I guess." She knew. She was glad she hadn't taken the folder from the car.

"Are you all right?" Mary's concern warmed her heart.

"Sure. It'll be over soon. It has to be. Where else could he search?" Kaylee glanced out the window at her car. It seemed so obvious to her.

Mary started for the door. "Ten minutes to touchdown. You should see the crowd. DeeDee's so excited her feet are barely touching the ground."

The bell over The Flower Patch's door jingled, and the three ladies who had been sitting in the front window of Death by Chocolate walked in.

"Look at this!" One stared at a grapevine wreath covered with dried flowers and berries, a little birdhouse, and a *Welcome* sign. "I have to have it."

Mary grinned at Kaylee. "It's a beautiful day in the neighborhood. See you later."

For the next hour business was heavy. Apparently people who came to see Ward Meacham or Lorelei Lewis came with the urge to buy. When Bea came in the door with Zoe on her heels, there was still a line at the cash register.

Bea slid behind the counter with Kaylee. "You can go over now. Zoe and I will handle everything until you come back."

Kaylee looked at Zoe doubtfully. The girl sidled up to a pair of women looking at some hand and body lotions and creams made by perfumers on Orcas.

"Doesn't that smell nice?" She squeezed a little from the sample bottle on her hands and rubbed it in. She sniffed and smiled. "My dad says it makes my mom smell good enough to eat."

The women looked at each other, then at Zoe who was still

smelling her hands, and each grabbed a bottle. Zoe looked at Kaylee and smiled like the little conspirator she was.

Kaylee had to laugh. "You're in good hands, Grandma. I'll be back soon."

"Take your time, sweetheart. There's a nice line over there."

When Kaylee walked into Between the Lines, she saw Bea wasn't exaggerating. Mary was at the register ringing up sales, and DeeDee flew around the store talking to customers, bringing beverages to those waiting in line, and suggesting other titles to interested readers.

Kaylee got in Ward's line, listening to the couple in front of her discussing the merits of Ward's latest book. She was surprised to hear their not-so-complimentary opinion reflect that of Lorie, which she'd given with glee the first night Kaylee met her. Was it only a few days ago Lorelei Lewis walked into her life?

Lorie's line for signatures might not be as long as Ward's, but it was certainly respectable. Many of the women in it had several of her books in their hands. Lorie was enjoying herself in full Lorelei mode as she hugged her readers and complimented each about something.

"Don't you have the cutest purse! Wherever did you find it?"

"Look at those earrings! They are so pretty on you."

She was wearing a vibrant caftan of sea greens and blues with huge earrings that matched and bangles on her arms that rattled musically as she signed.

Kaylee smiled at the tall, handsome man waiting for John Paul Jenkins in the line beside her. "Lorelei should give lessons on connecting with readers."

He looked at Lorie and smiled wistfully. "She loves every fan. Always has."

Interesting that a man knew so much about a romance author. It wasn't a guy's usual area of interest.

He offered Kaylee a solemn smile. "I'm excited to meet John Paul Jenkins. I love a good mystery."

*As well as a good romance? Or a good romance writer?*

As he turned his attention to the author seated before him, Kaylee noted the graying temples and handsome features. *Could it be?*

Finally it was Kaylee's turn with Ward. He glanced up with a practiced smile. "Hello. How are you?" Then he recognized her. "Kaylee! How wonderful of you to come." He stood and leaned over the table to kiss her cheek.

Suddenly Kaylee was a minor celebrity in her own right because Ward had singled her out. She flushed with pleasure.

"Here," he said. "I've got something to show you. Of course you might already know." He reached over the stack of his new title to snag a copy of *Never Too Late*, his first book and blockbuster best seller. He flipped the book open to the dedication page and read aloud, "To Porter Ashford and Edmond Lyons with thanks. I couldn't have done it without you."

Kaylee gasped and looked at the page. How had she never known this? She bit her lip against a wash of tears. "Did they ever know?"

His expression turned sad. "I don't think so. I know Porter didn't, and I don't think your grandfather did either. I was here for the Coterie and the book's launch when he disappeared. I'd sent him and your grandmother a special invitation to the launch party. I have always regretted I didn't have a chance to show him." A soft smile lit his face. "But I knew you'd like it."

"I think it's wonderful."

Ward flipped to the title page and signed the book with a great flourish, using one of his five requested markers. A young woman in New York black stood behind him with his new book opened to the title page in her hands, ready to pass it to him for signing. His tour handler? She gave Ward a little nudge in the shoulder with the corner of the book. Time to move to the next person in line. Both Kaylee and Ward ignored her.

Kaylee looked down at the signature and read, "To the beautiful Kaylee with much affection, Ward Meacham."

She felt herself flush with pleasure. She looked up at him and grinned. "You're good."

He laughed. "I try. See you later." Somehow he made it sound like a promise he was looking forward to keeping.

As she moved out of line, she caught Lorie's eye. "Wow!" Kaylee mouthed.

Lorie rolled her eyes.

Book in hand, Kaylee moved to the refreshment table where she balanced a cold glass of lemonade infused with lavender and one of Jessica's mini chocolate tarts on her book. She stepped into an aisle between two shelves of books and out of the main chaos as she took a bite. The chocolate was rich and dark and wonderful. Jessica had outdone herself. The lemonade was wonderful too, just the right sweet/tart ratio, and the elusive lavender—delicious.

The man who had been beside her in line and a young woman who looked vaguely familiar also stood in the aisle, glasses in hand.

"Next year I'll have a title to sign," the young woman told the man with pride and excitement in her tone. "Not that I'll have much of a line."

Kaylee realized she was looking at Shannon O'Mara, the young writer Lorie had invited to the Writers Coterie.

"I'm sure you'll do well," the man said with a kind smile.

"I signed my first contract with a New York house a couple of months ago." Shannon was trying so hard to be casual as she shared the news that Kaylee had to smile.

"Good for you," the man said. "Getting published traditionally is no easy task. The odds are against you."

"I had the recommendation of Lorelei Lewis to open a few doors. I'm so grateful."

"But you had to follow up her recommendation with a good story or it wouldn't have happened."

"Thanks. That's what I tell myself. I haven't heard yet if the publisher wants lots of edits, but Lorie—I mean Lorelei—said it was well done."

"If Lorie said it was well done, you may be sure it is. She's got an amazing ear for good writing." The man looked through the crowd to Lorie who was standing with a fan getting a selfie taken. "She's the best."

"You sound like you know her well," Shannon said. "Are you a writer too?"

"No, no, not me. I can barely put two sentences together." The man smiled again, this time with a touch of sadness. "But I've known Lorie for a long time." And he wandered off.

Kaylee watched him go, noticing he never took his eyes off Lorie for long. Was he who she thought he was?

"So you never knew, huh?"

Surprised, Kaylee turned to the woman with the raspy voice practically whispering in her ear. Somehow Roz Corzo didn't seem the book-signing sort. "Never knew what, Roz?"

"That he dedicated the book to Porter and Ed. I saw your smile when Howie showed it to you. You never knew." Today in honor of the signing she wore a too large, navy blazer that had seen better days—her late husband's?—over her baggy cords instead of her usual Corzo Whale Watch fleece.

"You're right. I didn't."

"I've always thought Howie had all the depth of a teaspoon, but that move impressed me. Made me reevaluate, you know?

Every time I read or hear anything about Howie on TV or in a magazine, it reminds me so much of Ed going out in his launch that last day, his old hat flopping in the breeze, his red coat flapping away."

"It was a very nice move . . . Wait." Kaylee stared at Roz. "What did you say?"

"It made me reevaluate."

"No. About my grandfather going out in his launch, not his skiff. It was his skiff they found floating in the Sound."

"Right. He took the launch to Deception Island that morning. He was looking for something special he wanted to tell you about. He came back disappointed. Then he stopped at Between the Lines, back when Milt Feinberg still owned it. I was coming out of the drugstore when Ed came out of the bookstore with a thoughtful expression and a copy of *Never Too Late*, which had just been released."

"He took the big boat," Kaylee repeated. "And wore the red jacket. You're sure?" She couldn't wait to tell her grandmother.

The first time he went out he took the launch—the big boat, yes. Then he took the skiff."

"He came home." No wonder the red barn jacket was still in the closet. No wonder Bea always pictured him going off wearing it. She wouldn't have seen him come home where he hung up the coat because she would have been working at The Flower Patch. Kaylee smiled as she pictured her grandmother's face when she told her.

The front door flew open, and Melanie Loblinski and her wedding party exploded into the store, laughing and waving.

"Hey, Mom!"

"Hey, Mrs. Loblinski! I mean Ms. Lewis."

The girls swarmed Lorie, getting hugs and lots of attention. "My daughter Melanie and her lovely friends!" Lorie told everyone before anyone could get angry at the girls' line jumping. "She's getting married this evening!"

Oohs and aahs filled the store along with numerous calls of, "She'll be a beautiful bride!" Melanie did look beautiful, her red hair shining, her aqua tunic making her eyes glow.

"And this is my dad who came all the way from New York to give me away!" Melanie pulled the handsome man who had been talking to Shannon forward. Kaylee smiled to herself. *So I was right.*

Calls for a family picture erupted as all Lorie's readers and many of Ward's pulled out their phones. Melanie stood between Dennis and Lorie as if there was no strain between the three. When Dennis's arm reached across Melanie's shoulder to rest on Lorie's shoulder, Kaylee noticed Lorie lean into his touch.

Wondering how Ward felt about the signing being co-opted so thoroughly, Kaylee glanced at him and caught the dagger of a look he threw Lorie's way. Professional jealousy was alive and well at Between the Lines.

Ward seemed to feel her watching him and turned. When he saw her, he erased the scowl and gave her a smoldering wink. She smiled back, thinking that the image consultant he'd told them about the other day had done a good job. Howie, the geek Bea remembered, was gone, and in his place was a practiced flirt and charmer, even if he did have a problem with the success of others.

Kaylee finished her lemonade, waved good-bye to DeeDee, and made her way back to The Flower Patch. When she entered, she noticed with pleasure that there were several empty spaces on the wall where wreaths had hung. Zoe was busily rearranging shelves to hide the fact that several items were missing.

Three cheers for Ward Meacham.

Kaylee and Bea spent the afternoon creating arrangements

and bouquets for the wedding using the combination of ordered flowers and wildflowers. Zoe watched with interest.

"What do you call that?" she asked, pointing to a peony.

"*Paeonia lactiflora.*"

"And that?"

"Shasta daisy," said Bea. "Don't put any in the bridal bouquet, Kaylee. The bride doesn't like daisies, remember?"

"*Leucanthemum superbum.* And don't worry, Grandma. I remember."

"If I'm a plant taxonomist, do I have to learn all those weird names?" Zoe asked.

"You do. Those weird names let scientists around the world know which plant someone is talking about, even if they speak a different language."

"What's this?" She held up a trail of deep green ivy.

"*Hederahelix,* commonly known as English ivy."

Zoe wrinkled her nose. "I think maybe I'll be a mathematician."

"An interesting possibility."

"Or a professional baseball player."

"Even more interesting."

After watching for a few more minutes, Zoe asked, "Why aren't you making all the bridesmaids' bouquets the same? On TV they're the same."

"Because we didn't know there were five bridesmaids until yesterday." Bea's voice was only slightly sour. "Therefore they have to take what they get. Can you roll that wastebasket over to me?"

"Sure. Can I sweep the leaves and stuff off the floor too?"

Kaylee smiled. "That's how I started, Zoe."

"This is more fun than sweeping up for my mom. She only has regular dust."

Slowly five colorful and unique bouquets took shape. As

Kaylee looked at the bursts of color in the cooler, she was proud of her work. Bea's bridal bouquet was a thing of beauty, with not a daisy in sight. Lorie's corsage and boutonnieres for Ryan, Dennis, and Reese joined the other flowers.

"Ryan has no parents?" Kaylee frowned as she realized there was no request for anything for his side of the family.

Bea shrugged. "You just make what's ordered and ask no questions."

Zoe eyed the few flowers left over. She ran a finger over a perky golden coreopsis. "Are you going to use these flowers?"

Kaylee glanced at her grandmother and they shared a smile. "I don't think so. Why?"

"It's just that I've been working all afternoon, and I'm not charging anything for my labor."

"And we've been so pleased to have the help."

"Right. So I was wondering . . ." Her voice trailed off, as she didn't have the courage to say what she wanted to say.

"You know what I was thinking?" Kaylee tried to look thoughtful. "I was thinking that it'd be fun to make corsages for you and your sister in honor of your first real wedding. That is, if you'd like one."

Zoe's smile lit up the room. Bea handed the corsages for the girls—each with its own big pearl-headed pin, each in its own box—to Zoe.

"I gotta show my mom!" And she was gone, running across the street with her eyes on the box instead of where she was going. Somehow she made it safely to Between the Lines.

"That was a great surprise for the girls, Grandma. I'm glad we had already made them up." Kaylee checked her watch. Four o'clock. "Reese bought several flats of impatiens and left them at the Ashford home. I'm going to run out there and make sure they're watered. Then I'll be back to help transport the flowers to our place."

"You go ahead. Reese took the arbor and a couple of the white wedding tables a while ago, and the rental company should have set up the chairs. Stop and check before you come back, will you?"

"Not a problem. Ride, Bear?"

The little dog looked up from the ball of crumpled tissue paper he'd been batting around the workroom and ran to the door. He tripped down the porch stairs and sat patiently while Kaylee fastened his safety vest. When they arrived at the Ashfords', he set to exploring the yard.

The impatiens were where Reese said they were, tucked under the overgrown boughs of the azaleas and rhododendron. The blooms would look colorful and cheerful planted across the front of the house. She checked the soil in the flats and went to the outside spigot to get water. She turned it, but nothing happened. The outside water hadn't been turned on.

She'd have to lug water from in the house—if she could get inside. She tried the front door even though she expected it to be locked. It was.

She didn't have time to go home and bring water today. She went back to check the flats to be certain she was comfortable waiting until tomorrow to give them water. Just as she decided she was, she noticed the poison hemlock was gone, pulled from its spot between two azaleas. The ground was still disturbed where it had been yanked out, root and all.

She looked around to see if Reese had just tossed it aside, worried Bear might find it and make himself sick or worse, but it was nowhere in sight. She hadn't seen Reese today, but her grandmother had said he'd been in the store for the arbor. He must have taken her advice about protective clothing to handle the hemlock or he'd be a sick guy.

She stepped back and surveyed the permanent plantings across the front of the house. She looked at the redbud tree and frowned. It looked out of place in the middle of the traditional foundation plantings. It would have been better placed to the far side as a sort of anchor planting rather than in the center where for half the year its bare branches would look sad among the evergreen leaves of the others.

*Make it look nice for sales purposes,* she reminded herself. That was all she had to do. Redesigning the plantings wasn't her responsibility.

"Come on, Bear. We've got to stop at home and check on things for the wedding tonight."

# 18

Finally it was evening, and Kaylee and Bear were ready for the nuptial festivities. He was wearing his formal black bow tie, and Kaylee was wearing her black lace cocktail dress. She gave them both a final check in the mirror before she left her room, ready for the mother of the bride to use for her final prepping.

"We look quite lovely, my furry but handsome friend," she told Bear. "I can't imagine a better-looking couple."

He gave a single bark in answer, one she chose to interpret as, "Absolutely."

Kaylee checked the backyard once again while Bear ran out to do a final nature call before the wedding. The white trellis with its rounded top, white tulle, and twinkle lights looked pretty against the meadow with its colored blooms. The white pedestals flanked the trellis and were topped with Bea's beautiful rainbow-colored arrangements. Fifty white chairs sat in five rows of ten each, an aisle with a red runner dividing them into a bride's side and a groom's side.

*Who*, Kaylee wondered, *will sit on the groom's side?*

Bright laughter drew her eyes to the bridesmaids and Melanie, who were getting their pictures taken while the sun was still strong. Their color-drenched bouquets looked wonderful against their soft yellow dresses. Even the muumuu looked pretty.

Ryan and Reese had been ordered to stay away from the house until fifteen minutes before the ceremony, which was to begin at 7:30. Couldn't let the groom see the bride too soon.

Lorie walked in still wearing the bright caftan she'd had on at the signing. Over her arm she carried the many-colored coat she'd worn the other day.

"In here." Kaylee showed her to her room.

Lorie walked in and sank onto the bed. "It's really going to happen, isn't it? I kept hoping I was going to wake up and find it's all a bad dream."

"I'm sorry, Lorie."

Lorie sighed deeply and held out the coat of many colors. "Since I didn't know I was going to be the mother of a bride, I didn't bring anything special to wear. Should I wear what I've got on or the coat?"

In Kaylee's opinion both were over-the-top wild and neither was the usual mother-of-the-bride outfit. "I thought the MOB was supposed to keep her mouth shut and wear beige."

"Ha! As if I'd ever wear beige. And that's the mother of the groom."

"Okay. That makes more sense."

"So which one?"

"You know, they both look good on you, and with Melanie as the bride, you could wear anything and you won't overshadow her. She's so beautiful."

Lorie's eyes softened. "She is, isn't she? She takes after her daddy's side of the family. She looks a lot like his mother." Lorie sighed. "I miss her. Best mother-in-law ever."

"I saw Dennis at the signing."

"How could you miss him with that trick Mellie pulled? Family pictures, my eye. I don't think I've ever acted so hard in my life, and that's considering I play Lorelei on a regular basis."

Kaylee patted her new friend's arm. "I know this is a tough weekend for you. You're doing fine."

Lorie took a deep breath. "So which one?"

"The coat. It's a little less, um, flamboyant."

"Really?" Lorie studied it.

"With the black slacks and shell, of course." Kaylee checked her watch. "Excuse me. I need to call the girls in so they're out of sight before guests begin arriving." Though who the guests would be was a great mystery.

"Everyone in the Coterie said they were coming. I need to tell Reese to seat them on the groom's side. The Petals and any curious locals or fans can sit on our side."

"I'll tell him." Lorie might bluster and speak her piece, sometimes unwisely, but she didn't want Ryan to have an empty side, even if she claimed she didn't like him. Kaylee was moved by her surprising generosity.

Kaylee left Lorie and called the wedding party women inside. She led them to Bea's room with its en suite bathroom for their last-minute primping. When she returned to the living room, Dennis Loblinski stood staring out the picture window at the ceremony venue, looking very suave in a gray suit and perfectly knotted tie, his boutonniere already in his lapel.

"I'm worried about her," he said.

Kaylee smiled. She liked the man. "I wouldn't be. Melanie's fine."

"I wasn't talking about Melanie."

Kaylee blinked. "Oh."

He bent to pet Bear who had been staring up at him in invitation. "She's here, isn't she?"

"Back in my bedroom. Come with me." She led him to her room, Bear bounding along beside them. They found Lorie still sitting on the bed looking glum. She didn't look up, though she must have heard them. Kaylee walked in and touched her shoulder.

"The coat, huh?" Lorie asked without enthusiasm. "Not the caftan?"

"The coat," Dennis said. "I've never seen you in it."

Lorie caught her breath and looked at her husband standing in the doorway. Her chin came up as she forced all traces of vulnerability away. "And whose fault is that?"

Dennis raised his hand, palm out. "Not today, Lorie, okay? Not today."

Lorie's shoulders slumped and when she spoke again, her voice was soft and sad. "Then when, Dennis? You've refused to talk to me for three years."

He pressed his lips together and looked like a giant, well-groomed rock that was not going to be moved.

"Sure. Stay silent." She began pacing, suddenly angry. "Make believe I don't deserve to know what's stuck in your craw!" She strode to him and poked him in the chest with enough force that he took a step back. "Have I ever told you I hate strong, silent types?"

Kaylee wanted nothing more than to leave the room. This wasn't a conversation she should be hearing, nor a confrontation she should be seeing. Bear leaned against her ankle, equally uneasy at the raised voices. Should she just excuse herself and walk out? But the door was blocked by the feuding parties—or party since Lorie seemed to be the only one itching for a fight.

"Excuse me, I think I should go." Kaylee took a step toward the door in the hope that one or both would move.

Lorie spun. "No, you'll stay right here as a witness. When I kill him, you can testify that I was provoked beyond endurance." She whirled back to Dennis in full diva mode. "Now talk!" And suddenly she was sobbing, her face crumpling as she buried it in her hands.

"Lorie!" Dennis reached for her, his face a study in concern and distress.

Kaylee expected Lorie to jump back, to push him away, but she didn't. She let him hold her as she wept. He murmured softly to her, rocking her gently. Kaylee sat on the bed and pretended she wasn't there.

As Lorie's tears lessened, Dennis pulled his handkerchief from his breast pocket and handed it to her, one arm still around her.

"Thanks," Lorie muttered. She ran her hand down the wet marks on his jacket. "Look what I did. And there's makeup on your shirt."

He shrugged. "I don't care. I got to hold you again."

She blew her nose and dabbed at her eyes. "Dennis, what happened? Please tell me."

Dennis looked despairing. "But you know."

"I don't. I really don't."

He took a deep breath. "Okay, if you say so. In a word, Ward."

"Ward?" Lorie looked flummoxed. "What's Ward got to do with anything?"

Dennis stiffened and took a step backward. His face hardened. "Do you deny it?"

"Deny what? There's nothing to deny."

"He's here, still hanging around you."

"Ward? He didn't come to Orcas until today. Right, Kaylee?"

Kaylee closed her eyes. Why this particular question when she'd be so happy being ignored? "Um, actually he's been here since Thursday at least."

"Really? I haven't seen him."

"Please," Dennis said. "Do I look like an idiot?"

"If you think there's anything between me and Ward Meacham, then yes, you are an idiot. I despise the man."

"There are pictures, Lorie." Pain etched Dennis's face. "How can you argue with pictures?"

Her head snapped back in surprise. "Pictures of what?"

"Pictures of you and Ward. The two of you together. Cozy pictures. The kind that make you look like a couple."

Lorie shook her head. "No. No, no, no, no! I don't even like the man. He's smarmy and phony and talentless."

"But the pictures! It's definitely you. And him."

"Someone must have edited them digitally."

He grabbed his phone and pushed some buttons. "Here." He held it out to her.

Lorie looked at it incredulously. "That rat! That dirty rat. I'm going to kill him." She took a deep breath and forced herself to calm down. "It's a fake, Dennis. In the real picture, I was sitting next to Porter."

Dennis blinked. "But he's been dead for years."

"The picture's old." Her red nail poked the phone screen. "I don't even look like that anymore. I'm twenty pounds heavier, and my hair's not even the same color."

Dennis frowned down at the photo, then looked up at Lorie in confusion.

"In the real picture, Porter had just told me how proud he was of me and my success. I laid my head on his shoulder for a minute. It was like a daughter showing affection to her father. You know how I loved Porter. And if everyone hadn't been digitally erased, the other Coterie members would be sitting with us. I certainly wouldn't rest my head on Ward's shoulder under any circumstances." She shuddered.

"But what about this?" He pulled up a second picture. "This was from a couple of months ago, when I was thinking about coming back anyway."

Lorie snorted. "We were at an awards gala. He came up behind me and wrapped his arms around my waist before I saw him coming. What could I do but laugh with all those people watching? He had me and he knew it. He snuggled in and leaned forward and gave me a kiss on the cheek. I thought I was going to be sick." Lorie made a face. "The picture was in *People*."

"The Career Achievement Award you won and he didn't?"

"The very same." She looked at him. "How do you know about that?"

"I try to keep up with you."

Kaylee wondered if they realized they were standing shoulder to shoulder, touching all down one side of their bodies, as they looked at Dennis's phone.

"Who sent you these pictures, Dennis?"

"I don't know. They just come. Every time I tell myself to get over my jealousy and fight for you, another shows up."

"For three years?"

"For three years."

"It's Ward. I can't prove it, but I know it is."

Dennis looked at his phone again. "Why?"

"Spite. He's a sick man who's jealous of other people's success. If he can't ruin their career, he tries to ruin them in other ways. My readers don't care what he says, so he has to go after the private me. And he knew the best way to destroy me was to take you away from me."

"I don't . . ." His voice trailed off.

Lorie patted him on the chest. "You don't understand meanness and spite. That is what you're trying to say. You're a good, honorable man."

"Naïve." He looked embarrassed.

"Maybe a bit. You would never do something so despicable as to try to ruin someone's marriage, so you can't imagine anyone else doing it. You accepted the photos at face value."

"I didn't know what to think. On one hand there were the pictures and then the don't-try-to-contact-me e-mails."

"What no-contact messages? I only ever wanted you to come back."

He put his hand over hers, still resting on his chest. "On

the other hand, you were saying call me, talk to me. I was so confused and hurt I just buried myself in my business, traveling overseas three out of every four weeks because I didn't know how to deal with it all." He smiled sadly. "Not what one of your heroes would do, is it? Can you ever forgive me?"

"My heroes aren't real, Dennis. You're real."

The door of the bedroom where the girls were doing their final primping for the wedding flew open. Kaylee jumped to her feet. As *de facto* wedding coordinator, she had to get out there to do her job. Unfortunately Dennis and Lorie still blocked the doorway, though their attention was snagged by the girls.

One by one the young women in yellow walked out.

Lorie clapped her hands. "Ladies, you look wonderful!" She and Dennis moved toward the girls, and finally Kaylee escaped the bedroom, Bear at her heels.

Then Melanie walked out, looking radiant and excited.

"Oh, honey!" Lorie rushed to her daughter with her arms wide.

"No kisses, Mom." Melanie held a hand out. "I don't want to walk down the aisle with a big lip print on my cheek." But she said it with a smile.

Lorie laughed and hugged her daughter. Dennis watched his women, an adoring look on his face. He kissed Melanie, stepped back and slipped an arm around Lorie.

Melanie looked from one to the other of her parents, her face full of hope. "Are you two doing okay?"

Dennis and Lorie looked at each other. "Better than okay," Lorie said.

"Can you wait a minute before you go out to Ryan?" Dennis asked. "Your mom wants to change her dress."

"Sure," Melanie said. "It's not like Ryan's going anywhere."

Lorie moved to close the bedroom door, then stopped.

Almost shyly, she stood on tiptoe and kissed Dennis. Then she ducked back into Kaylee's bedroom and shut the door, leaving Dennis standing outside, his face as radiant as any lovestruck young boy's.

Kaylee groped at her empty pockets as her eyes stung with happy tears. Where was a tissue when you needed one?

# 19

The wedding was lovely. A surprising number of people came, the chairs almost all taken. Zoe and Polly watched with shining eyes, their corsages swallowing their small shoulders. The Coterie gave Ryan's side of the aisle an impressive cachet. Reese looked very handsome standing beside Ryan and performed his best man duties well.

To Kaylee's surprise Nick Durham came, wearing a dress shirt and slacks instead of his uniform. She smiled at him and he almost smiled back. Did that mean she was almost forgiven for her silence?

Melanie looked stunning, her eyes aglow as she promised to love Ryan with her whole heart, encourage him to reach for his dreams, and respect him as her partner in life. Ryan read the vows he had written in a loud, clear voice, promising to love her as himself, protect her from life's storms, and provide for her as long as they lived.

The maturity of the vows and the fact that Ryan could actually speak—and speak with spirituality and wisdom no less—made Kaylee think for the first time that the marriage might actually work out.

The reception dinner at the Turtle Cove Inn was a happy occasion. Melanie and Ryan couldn't stop grinning and held hands the whole time, which made for some awkward eating. Lorie was so caught up in her own joy with Dennis that she forgot to carp about Ryan. Reese and Nick, as the sole available males present, were very popular with the bridesmaids in spite of the twenty-year age difference.

Ward, in attendance with the rest of the Coterie, was his charming public persona when he wasn't glaring surreptitiously at Lorie and Dennis. He seemed particularly interested in charming Kaylee.

"You look beautiful tonight, Kaylee." He leaned in to kiss her cheek. "I would be honored if you'd sit with me for dinner."

Feeling trapped by this man she now considered reprehensible, she didn't know what to do. "I can't sit with the Coterie. I'm not a member."

"But you'll be my guest." His smile was warm and admiring, and if she didn't know what he really was, she'd have been swept away by the attention.

"Kaylee! Over here!"

Kaylee saw Lorie and Dennis motioning her to their table. Her grandmother already sat there with Jessica and DeeDee and the girls. There was one seat left.

"Thanks so much, Ward, but I'm supposed to sit over there." She gave a little laugh which sounded strained and brittle to her ears. "Can't stand up my grandmother or the parents of the bride on their big day. You sit with the Coterie. I'll sit with the Petals."

And she fled, making believe she didn't see the angry thundercloud that rolled across his face before he gave a curt nod of acknowledgment.

He stayed long enough to eat and look down his nose at everyone. The Coterie members with whom he sat seemed to give a collective sigh of relief when he left without waiting for the cutting of the cake—which was lovely and made Bea laugh, frosted as it was with yellow and white daisies.

As he cast a final surly look back before disappearing into the dark, Lorie waved to him, her smile big and bright. Then she leaned over and kissed Dennis.

Finally the party ended, and Kaylee and Bea returned to Wildflower Cottage, exhausted but happy.

"I'm getting too old for this." Bea leaned on the kitchen counter as if walking the few steps to her bedroom was more than she could handle. "I've got to get to Arizona before I wear myself out."

Kaylee cast a worried glance at her grandmother. "Want a cup of chamomile tea to help you sleep?"

Bea straightened. "Absolutely not. No more liquids! I'll be up at all times of the night as it is. And it's a good tired, sweetheart. Don't worry so much."

"Love you, Grandma." With a happy heart, Kaylee went to her bedroom. In a few minutes she was leaning back against her pillows, her laptop open before her. She only had the last three chapters to read in Porter's book. She was dying to see if it ended as she thought it would.

A short while later she closed her laptop, a smile on her lips. Things in Riley's world weren't always happy, but they were always grace-filled and right. Both Riley and his grandfather finished well in spite of the chaos of the war years and the uncertainties inherent in growing up and growing old.

For a few minutes she sat, basking in the wonder of it all. She hated to lose the magic of Riley's world.

Her eyes felt droopy. She should slide down under the covers and give in to the fatigue of a long and satisfying day. Bea was going to the nine o'clock service at her church and then out to brunch with friends, and Kaylee was going with them. She could sleep until eight. She couldn't even remember the last time she'd slept that late. She stretched and smiled contentedly.

Her eyes fell on *Never Too Late*, sitting on the nightstand. She grabbed it, opened to the title page, and read Ward's lovely inscription. *To the beautiful Kaylee.* Her lip curled. *Liar, liar, pants on fire.*

She remembered how impressed and excited she'd been just a few hours ago when he had written those words. Now she knew Lorie was right. He was smarmy and phony and just plain mean.

She flipped to the dedication page and ran her finger over her grandfather's name. Convinced now that Ward did everything out of self-interest, she wondered about the inscription. *I couldn't have done it without you.* What was the double-edged meaning of the words?

She flipped to page one of Ward Meacham's book and read, *Riley Morgan did not know what to believe.*

Kaylee slapped her hand over her mouth in horror. She didn't know what to believe either. Well, she did. It was just that she couldn't believe it. She read on, flipping pages and checking the story's progression.

Ward Meacham was a plagiarist! He was a cheat and a liar of unbelievable gall. He'd built his entire career on the work of Porter Ashford. No wonder his later books hadn't lived up to his early promise.

But where had he gotten Porter's book? How had he gotten it?

She sat up straight. Gone was any thought of sleep, and questions and possible conclusions flew through her mind at warp speed. Bear felt her movement and looked up groggily.

"It's okay, Bear." She reached down and petted him. "Go back to sleep."

With a sigh and a yawn, he obeyed.

Kaylee narrowed her eyes, her mind racing as she reviewed everything she remembered about Ward and Porter. Ward, then Howie, came to Orcas to be mentored by Porter. Ward had big dreams, but Porter had little hope for him. Ward found Porter's body.

That last detail was important somehow. She knew it. So was that eerily neat office.

Had Ward gone through Porter's office before he called 911? The thought made her shudder, but it made sense. If he was to claim *Never Too Late* as his work, he had to be certain there was no evidence of the book left anywhere. Had he e-mailed the manuscript to himself as an attachment and then wiped it from Porter's computer, not realizing there was that black wastebasket in the deep desk kneehole or the thumb drive fallen behind the books?

Seven years ago, Porter died.

Five years ago *Never Too Late* was released. Give the normal two-year process for a traditionally published book to go from agent to contract to writing and editing to release, the math worked.

She thought of the calculation Ward had shown in trying to sabotage Lorie's and Dennis's marriage, and all because she was a more successful writer than he. How it must have galled him when she won that award he had so coveted. How he must have resented Porter, this man who also had the great success Ward felt he deserved. In his mind, Porter wouldn't do for him what he'd done for Lorie and others.

A chill swept over Kaylee as another thought occurred. Did Ward have anything to do with Porter's death? Did he guarantee his own access to the manuscript by killing the real author?

She massaged her temples as if the action would stimulate her memory. Fact one: Porter was found in his front hall at the bottom of his stairs to the second floor. Fact two: Ward Meacham, then Howie, found him.

Question one: Did Ward help him fall?

The problem with this scenario was that there was no guarantee that a shove down the stairs would kill someone. Hurt, yes. Kill? Only maybe.

Question two: Was an autopsy conducted, and if so, what were its findings? Since Porter was presumed to have died alone, the medical examiner or his authorized deputy would have had to declare death. Presumably the medical examiner in Seattle then would have performed an autopsy to determine cause of death, especially for someone as prominent as Porter Ashford. Bea would know if one had been performed and what the results were.

Goosebumps sprang up all over her body as another thought occurred. Ward had dedicated *Never Too Late* to Porter and Kaylee's grandfather. *I couldn't have done it without you.*

Ed had gotten his first look at the published book the day he died if Roz's version of things was accurate. But what if Porter followed the pattern he'd followed with his fantasy novels? Had he used Kaylee's grandfather as a first reader of the manuscript as he wrote it? Had he discussed Riley at their Wednesday night dinners? If her grandfather was familiar with the story, what a shock he must have had when he read that first line.

Apparently Grandpa knew about the plagiarism for several days before his death if she understood the journal entries correctly. Had Grandpa somehow gotten hold of an excerpt? Read a review that gave plot details? Then he got a copy of the book which confirmed all his suspicions.

Had he gone to confront Ward at Mermaid Cottage?

*Stop! Slow down, Kaylee.*

She was getting carried away. It was a long jump from plagiarism to assuming confrontation and murder.

She lay back against her pillows. She knew two things: She wasn't going to sleep tonight, and she couldn't wait to talk things over with Isaac, then Nick.

# 20

She awoke from a restless and unexpected sleep at six, nerves strung as tight as an orchestra's kettledrum. Going back to sleep was impossible. She got up and threw on an old pair of jeans and a T-shirt. Coffee. She needed caffeine.

As she waited for the coffee to brew, she paced the kitchen. Bear sat beside the island and watched her, clearly perplexed by her agitation.

"Just ignore me, Bear. I'm okay."

He decided to believe her and went to munch his breakfast.

In moments she poured the hot, fragrant coffee into a travel mug and sipped as she paced. She needed something to occupy her mind until she could meet with Isaac.

"Come on, Bear. Let's go water the impatiens. Then we won't have to worry about them for the rest of the day."

Bear hadn't planned to worry about the flowers in any case, but he followed her happily outside and nosed at the edges of the yard for evidence of new creatures that had happened by overnight. Kaylee filled a bucket with water and loaded it in the floor well between the front and back seats, wedged in with pillows like before.

The morning mist lay in the meadows as they drove the short distance to the Ashford place. Sunlight streaked through the canopy of leaves in the forested stretch of road, and she thought vaguely that they looked like golden ribbons against the rich, green backdrop.

Bear jumped to the ground as soon as he was released from his harness and began exploring. Kaylee opened the back door to retrieve the water and noticed the pruning shears lying on the backseat, left from her collecting of wildflowers for the wedding. She heard her grandmother's words from her childhood: "Always clean and care for your tools, Kaylee. They deserve it and will perform better for you if you do."

She grabbed the clippers and stuck the blades down in the back pocket of her jeans so she couldn't forget them and their cleaning when she got back home.

She lugged the bucket of water to the edge of the front garden, and using the cup she'd brought, began watering the thirsty impatiens. She'd barely begun when she heard a car pull up. She straightened, expecting to see Reese in his black pickup come to work on the house.

Instead Ward Meacham stepped from his rental car. Her palms turned clammy and her stomach decided it didn't like coffee. She swallowed the rush of acid.

"Good morning, Kaylee. I was hoping to see you alone." He smiled that ingratiating smile that now repulsed her. No, make that frightened her. She did not like the idea of being here alone with him now that she was pretty sure she knew what he'd done, especially since no one knew she was here.

"Hi, Ward." She tried to seem casual, friendly. "I've come to water the impatiens so I can forget them for the rest of the day." Her voice sounded a bit breathy from nerves.

"You have a busy day planned?"

*Yes. I'm going to the police about you.* "I'm going to church with my grandma and then out for brunch with her and her friends. I actually need to be getting back soon."

"Isn't that nice."

She forced herself not to respond to the snide note in his voice. She continued to water the impatiens, anxious to get her errand finished so she could get far away from him.

He moved toward her with a strange intensity. In his hands he held a travel mug. "How did you like *Never Too Late?*"

She blinked at the unexpected question. Was he testing her? "Yesterday was a busy day, so I only got to read a couple of pages before I fell asleep. It's going to be good. I can tell."

She hoped he'd buy that line. She wasn't a good liar. Of course that wasn't really a lie. She had read only a few pages of his book—enough to know that he'd stolen it from Porter. Of course she loved Porter's book.

She dumped the last of the water on the last impatiens. She gripped her bucket and prepared to flee to her car.

"Don't you just love this redbud, Kaylee?" He was beside her, staring at the leafy tree, a few of its tiny mauve blossoms still clinging to the branches.

Again an unexpected question. "*Cercis canadensis*. It looks a little out of place where it is. I would have put it over there." She pointed to the corner of the house.

"Probably a better place, though the soil is bound to make for rough digging there." He shrugged. "Too late now."

She started toward her car. "Maybe the new owners will move it."

"That would be interesting." He followed her. "Did you know the redbud is sometimes called the Judas tree?"

"The legend says Judas hanged himself on a species of redbud, the *Cercis siliquastrum*, a cousin of this tree. Its blooms were once white, the legend goes, but it blushed to be part of such a terrible history."

"The tree of a traitor." He smiled, all teeth and pride.

Kaylee shivered. Traitors did not live only in Jesus's time. "Come here, Bear. We have to go."

"Why the hurry, pretty Kaylee? There's plenty of time until church."

She indicated her T-shirt and jeans. "And I need every moment to get presentable."

He looked her up and down. "You did look prettier yesterday." He held out his mug. "Want a drink?"

"Uh, no thanks. I have my own in the car." She felt twitchy with tension. "Come, Bear." Her voice was sharp.

"You want a drink." It was an order.

Kaylee looked at him, startled. "No."

He brought the mug up to her chin. "Drink."

Kaylee caught her breath when she realized he'd backed her against the car. "No, I don't want a drink." She put up a hand.

He ignored her and pushed the cup at her. She recoiled, and as she did, she caught the mousy scent of the beverage. She'd read the phrase *mousy scent* many times and never been quite sure what it meant, but she knew now. Her gaze went without thought to the disturbed soil where the poison hemlock had been.

He followed her eyes and gave a half laugh. "So you know."

"*Conium maculatum.*"

He smiled. "Is that its fancy name? Impressive you know it."

"Not really. It's my field."

"Drinking it was how Socrates was executed for corrupting the youth of his day." He continued to smile, but it didn't reach his eyes.

"That's what you get for teaching kids to think."

Ward didn't respond to her crack. He was too intent on the history of the plant. "His most famous student, Plato, wasn't with him when he died, but Plato described his death from eyewitness accounts. He said it was by paralysis and started at the legs and worked its way up the body. Socrates died when it reached his respiratory system."

Kaylee shivered. "A gruesome way to go."

"Not really. Plato said it was painless. He said Socrates's mind was alert until the very end."

Kaylee looked at the travel mug in his hand, still much too close to her face.

Meacham continued. "You die from the outside in. None of the seizures and cramping of other poisons." He looked thoughtful. "I think Plato was right. At least that's been my experience."

The hairs on the back of her neck stood up at what he implied.

"Here. Have a drink or two and we'll do another experiment."

Again the mousy smell associated with *Conium maculatum* assaulted her. She reached behind her for her door handle. If she could get inside the car and lock the door, she could get away.

"Bear? Where are you?" She couldn't go anywhere without her boy.

He came running from the side yard where he was exploring and sat beside her. She glanced down and saw his worried little face. He felt the tension bathing the atmosphere even if he didn't understand it. He sat as close to her feet as he could without sitting on them.

Ward pressed her against the car, catching her arm behind her as she reached for the door handle, squashing the tender flesh painfully.

Bear came to his feet with a growl. He showed his teeth and his hackles rose.

Ward glanced down and sneered. He turned back to Kaylee. "When did you figure it out?"

There was no use pretending she didn't know what he was talking about. "Last night. I suspected something strange before, but I knew last night."

"You have that missing folder."

"You're the one who cleaned the house and removed all the wastebaskets so no one could find something that would indicate your work wasn't yours," she retorted. "But you missed a couple of spots. How long after you 'found' Porter did it take for you to call the police, Howie? And you've been tearing apart people's homes. You hired that guy to send me that bouquet, hoping I'd get scared enough to get rid of the folder."

"My, you have been working hard, haven't you? You must be thirsty. Drink." He thrust the mug at her.

Bear snarled and lunged for Ward, snapping at his ankles. Ward kicked out. Bear dodged and came at him from the rear.

"Get that animal out of here!"

Kaylee ignored him and pressed her lips together, curling them inward and clamping her teeth for extra protection. At the same time, she swung the bucket still dangling from her arm. She only needed to distract him for a second.

Ward saw the missile coming just before it connected and shifted so it caught him on the shoulder instead of the head as she had wanted. "Why you—" Fury made the vein in his forehead pulse and his face turn scarlet.

She tried to pull the bucket back for another swing, but he grabbed it by the lip and yanked. The force of the pull not only ripped the bucket from her hand but threw her against him.

"No!" She jumped away, coming up against her car again. Now she held her hands out in front of her.

Ward laughed and tossed the bucket into the foundation plantings. "You don't want any tea, Kaylee? Maybe your dog would like some."

She looked at Bear who was barking wildly as he continued to snap at Ward. "Run, Bear! Run!"

Bear grabbed Ward's pant leg and shook.

Ward kicked out, sending Bear flying. He landed with a grunt.

"Bear!" Kaylee jumped at Ward. "You leave him alone!"

Ward grabbed her arm and bent it behind her. Bear came

running at him again. Laughing, Ward tipped the mug so liquid spilled onto the grass.

"No!" Kaylee stuck out a foot to stop Bear who froze at the terror in her voice.

Ward sneered. "Like you could protect him if I want him."

She glared defiantly at Ward. Nobody was hurting her baby! "Stay back, Bear! Stay back!"

The dog looked up at her, uncertain. Then Ward pushed her back against the car, and Bear went into protective mode again, snarling and barking and attacking.

Ward sneered. "Softhearted, clever Kaylee. Trying to save her beloved pet but losing herself." He grabbed her face, fingers and thumb straddling her mouth, and pressing, pressing into her cheeks, tried to force her mouth open.

"No little prissy princess is taking away what I've built for myself." His breathing was rapid, his eyes wild. "You can fight me all you want, but I'll win. I beat your grandfather. I'll best you."

She glared at him. Not if she could help it.

Ward gave a bark of laughter. "Old Ed came so self-righteously to confront me. 'Howie, what have you done?' Only I was no longer Howie, a fact he didn't understand. I was Ward. 'Sit, Ed,' I said. 'Let's have lunch while we talk this through.' I was ready for him if he came. He and Porter were such friends. I knew about his being first reader for the fantasies. I suspected it for *Never Too Late*."

Kaylee saw it all, the salad with poison hemlock leaves among the greens, maybe its tubers cut among the vegetables, a strong salad dressing to cover that mousy scent.

She fumbled behind her again for the door handle. As she did, she felt the shears in her back pocket.

She had her mouth clamped as firmly closed as possible, but the force of his fingers was having an effect. It was only a matter of time before he would be able to pour that poisoned tea down her throat.

He leaned close, the better to torment her. "No one beats me, Kaylee. No one. Not Porter Ashford, not your beloved grandfather, and certainly not a pathetic little botanist like you."

Bear barked and lunged, his sharp little teeth finally making contact with Ward's ankles. Ward started and pulled back, kicking out. He let go of Kaylee and grabbed for Bear who, still growling, scuttled behind Kaylee.

Kaylee's fingers closed firmly over the handles of the clippers. She slid the tool from her back pocket and flicked off the lock. The blades sprang open, and she swung as hard as she could in a great sideways arc.

He screamed and dropped the mug as he staggered back, staring in disbelief at the clippers sticking from his thigh.

Kaylee grabbed Bear, opened the Escape's door, and tossed him in. Her back prickled in expectation of a hand grabbing her even as she dived into the car after him. She pulled the door shut and hit the lock. Bear climbed over her to snarl at Ward through the window.

"You are my brave boy!" She gave him a quick hug and put him back in the passenger seat. She turned the key. She took one last look at Ward just as he pulled the blades free. Blood ran freely down his leg. With grim satisfaction, she hit the gas.

# 21

Kaylee grabbed her phone and called Nick as she sped toward home. "Nick! You've got to go to the Ashfords' and arrest Ward Meacham!"

"What?"

She rounded a curve and Bear slid across the seat, scrabbling to avoid hitting the door.

"Sorry, buddy." She reached out and steadied him.

"What did you just say?"

"I was talking to Bear."

"No, before that."

"Oh, of course. Ward Meacham just tried to kill me."

"Are you in danger now?" he demanded.

"No. I got away. I stabbed him."

"You stabbed him?" This time it was disbelief traveling down the line.

"With a pair of very pointy English secateurs. But it was self-defense."

"Of course."

"He was trying to make me drink poison hemlock! What was I supposed to do? Say, 'Please, Ward, don't?'"

"Poison hemlock? How do you know?"

"There was a plant growing right in the Ashfords' garden and it's gone now. Ask Reese. He saw it too. And it smelled."

"You can identify hemlock by its smell?"

"Yes, it smells mousy. I have a PhD in plant taxonomy, remember?" Kaylee gulped. "And Nick—he killed my grandfather. And probably Mr. Ashford too."

"Slow down, Kaylee. Slow down."

She took her foot off the accelerator.

"Now start at the beginning."

So she did, starting with the red folder and its contents right up to speeding away from the bleeding Ward. "And check under the redbud tree. I think it's my grandfather's grave."

Six hours later Kaylee sat on Bea's patio with Reese, Nick, and Isaac Ashford. It had been a nail-biting few hours as she waited for news.

"Your call gave the Coast Guard the time they needed to find Ward Meacham, Kaylee." Nick leaned against the rail of the patio, badge gleaming in the sunshine. "They caught him in the Strait of Juan de Fuca, heading for Canada in the nifty cruiser he'd bought with a nice chunk of his book and movie money."

Reese leaned forward in his chair, elbows resting on his knees. "It was a beauty of a boat. Made yours look like a toy, Kaylee."

"A lot of the income from my dad's intellectual property will have been spent and is gone," Isaac said. "As for the rest, it'll take years to figure out all the financial and legal ramifications of Howie's actions."

"Forensic accountants will follow the money trail, even to offshore and foreign banks," Nick said. "If it's still out there, they'll find it."

"I feel sad that Porter never knew about the success of his book." Bea stared out over the meadow. "He would have so enjoyed it."

"I put in a call to his agent a couple of hours ago," Isaac said. "He said we should hold onto our hats because the story of the theft and murders will make it the must-have book all over again. And under my father's name this time."

Nick held up a cautionary hand. "Easy on saying murders, plural, Isaac. We don't know about your father, and I doubt we ever will. He may have fallen naturally or he may have been pushed."

"Or he could have been poisoned." Isaac let his anger show.

"That's doubtful since it didn't show up on the toxicology tests taken at the time of the autopsy. They were looking for drugs that might have caused him to fall." Nick shrugged. "There's no way to know unless Meacham decides to tell us, and I doubt he will."

"I'm sure he will. He loves taking credit for things." Kaylee shivered in spite of the warmth of the day. "He bragged to me as he was trying to kill me."

"One thing we know for sure," Nick said. "Meacham will be charged with Ed Lyons's murder and Kaylee's attempted murder, as well as fraud and theft and several other offenses. Even if we aren't able to connect him with your father's death, Isaac, he'll still spend the rest of his life behind bars."

*Ed Lyons's murder.* When Nick said the ugly words, Kaylee reached to her grandmother and took her hand. Bea smiled sadly and spoke for the first time in a while.

"You know, I hate knowing Ed was murdered, but I'm so relieved to finally know what happened and that justice will be served. Not knowing eats at you and taints everything. Now I can have a graveside service for Ed, a proper closing to his life. I can go to Tucson to live with Lucille, my life on Orcas having all its ends tied up."

"Like any good book." Kaylee leaned over and kissed Bea. "I'm going to miss you!"

"And I you, believe me. It's a good thing planes fly south so you can come and visit."

Kaylee sat back, enjoying the beauty and serenity of the meadow beyond the yard after the violence of the day. She looked at handsome, charming Nick who gave her a wink and made her grin in spite of the grimness of the day's occurrences. She thought of the Petals—DeeDee, Jessica, and Mary—and their all-for-one spirit. And then there was Reese, not only handsome but warm and friendly. He might not wink, but he still made her heart flutter.

Her life here was going to be full and rich, she just knew it. With the problems of the past few days solved, she could relax—at least for a few hours. Then the reality of owning The Flower Patch would come knocking at her door once again.

She lifted her face to the sun. Life on Orcas Island couldn't be sweeter.

## Up to this point, we've been doing all the writing. Now it's *your* turn!

Tell us what you think about this book, the characters, the bad guy, or anything else you'd like to share with us about this series. We can't wait to hear from *you!*

Log on to give us your feedback at:
**https://www.surveymonkey.com/r/FlowerShopMysteries**

*Annie's*® FICTION